Song Book

21 Songs from 10 Years (1964-1974)

Fiona McQuarrie

NEW HAVEN PUBLISHING

Published 2018
New Haven Publishing Ltd
www.newhavenpublishingltd.com
newhavenpublishing@gmail.com

All Rights Reserved
The rights of Fiona McQuarrie, as the author of this work, have been asserted in accordance with the Copyrights, Designs and Patents Act 1988.
No part of this book may be re-printed or reproduced or utilized in any form or by any electronic, mechanical or other means, now unknown or hereafter invented, including photocopying, and recording, or in any information storage or retrieval system, without the written permission of the Author and Publisher.

Cover design © Andy Morten
andymorten@mac.com

Copyright © 2018 Fiona McQuarrie
All rights reserved
ISBN: 978-1-912587-15-5

TABLE OF CONTENTS

Introduction	5
Every Time You Walk in the Room (Jackie DeShannon, 1964)	9
Iko Iko (The Dixie Cups, 1964)	15
Morning of My Life/In the Morning (The Bee Gees, 1965)	21
Sunny Goodge Street (Donovan, 1965)	27
Reason to Believe (Tim Hardin, 1966)	32
A Place in the Sun (Stevie Wonder, 1966)	38
Wasn't It You (Goffin & King/Petula Clark, 1966)	44
The First Cut is the Deepest (Cat Stevens/P.P. Arnold, 1967)	50
The Worst That Could Happen (Jimmy Webb/ The 5th Dimension, 1967)	56
Living Without You (Randy Newman, 1968)	62
I'm The Urban Spaceman (Bonzo Dog Doo-Dah Band, 1968)	68
Feelin' Alright (Traffic/Joe Cocker, 1968)	75
Think of Rain (Margo Guryan, 1968)	80
Abergavenny (Marty Wilde/Shannon, 1969)	86
Neanderthal Man (Hotlegs, 1970)	92
Lovin' You Ain't Easy (Michel Pagliaro, 1971)	99
Everything Stops for Tea (Long John Baldry, 1972)	106
You Put Something Better Inside Me (Stealers Wheel, 1972)	112
Sail On Sailor (The Beach Boys, 1973)	118
129/Matinee Idyll (Split Enz, 1973)	125
The True Wheel (Eno, 1974)	131
Bibliography	137
Acknowledgements	155
About the Author	156

INTRODUCTION

The seeds of this book were planted in 1967.

That year was memorable for many reasons, but in my corner of the world – Vancouver, Canada – it was an especially exciting time because of the rising recognition of Canadian music. Canada celebrated its 100th birthday in 1967, and the resulting sense of national identity and pride led to the realization that Canadian musicians didn't become successful only by going to the United States and becoming stars there. Canadians could love and support Canadian musicians and make them famous ourselves, without needing validation from our larger neighbour to the south.

So when a Vancouver-based musician named Tom Northcott released a magical record called 'Sunny Goodge Street', to my nine-year-old ears it was just a fantastic song that was even more special because it was made by a fellow Canadian (one from my own province too!). At some point I might have dimly understood that the song was actually written by Donovan, but I knew him mostly as the curly-haired guy with the odd accent who sang 'Sunshine Superman', a popular song among the hippies. In my world, hippies were my friends' slightly scary older brothers and sisters, who wore weird clothes and grooved to lyrics that I sensed had different meanings for bigger and more worldly kids. But I loved the lilting waltz of 'Sunny Goodge Street' as it rose up and down, up and down, like a carousel horse accompanied by a slightly wheezy, off-kilter organ.

For some reason - I can't honestly remember why or how - as I grew older, along with being interested in music, I became fascinated by musical trivia and by albums and singles charts. My bookshelves gradually became weighed down by chart compilations and other books of musical obscurities, and I started what I suppose was record collecting by buying oddities that no one else at the record store seemed to want. My interest in music led me to work for a few years as a music writer at a daily newspaper and then as a freelancer. Even after my professional interests evolved in different directions, the weird books and weird records stayed with me, and I acquired even more along the way.

Fast forward to early September 2015. It's late, it's dark, it's a hot late summer night, and I'm in my office at home pretending to work when up on my Facebook feed pops a post from *Shindig!*, a British music magazine that I'd grown to love over the past few years. "We're thinking of adding content to the website to supplement what's in the magazine. Are you interested in writing for us?" I hadn't written anything about music for more than two decades, but that post struck a chord with me. A few weeks earlier, I had published a work-related article in a national newspaper, really for no other reason than one of my friends had done the same and I thought, "If he can do that, so can I." I'd also recently started writing a blog about news and issues related to my professional interests, and no one had said "You stink, get off the Internet" – in fact, the blog had resulted in connections that opened up other opportunities. And yeah, if I'm being honest, I have to admit that I had just read a book about "the power of yes". Although I skipped through a lot of the book because it was so overwritten, its message reminded me of something I learned during my time as a theatre student. When doing improvisation, you never say "no" to what another actor does or suggests – you say "yes" and react to how things unfold from there.

One of the ideas that *Shindig!* proposed in its Facebook message was a feature called Story of a Song – an article that would be about a single song, its history, its cover versions, its successes or failures. I had a mind full of useless musical trivia, I had a shelf full of books about music, and I had just had some success saying "yes" to things I never would have thought I could do. So I figured, "Hey, I can do that." (If you know the musical *A Chorus Line*, the song 'I Can Do That' was madly running through my head at this point.)

I sent a Facebook message in response to the post, and struck up an email correspondence with *Shindig!*'s editors, Jon "Mojo" Mills and Andy Morten. The song I suggested for a Story of a Song feature, and which they agreed to, was my old friend 'Sunny Goodge Street'. I plundered YouTube, Discogs, and the Second Hand Songs website – none of which even existed the last time I had written about music – put together an article, held my breath, and hit 'send'. Jon and Andy liked the article enough to run it in the magazine, in a feature they titled "Song Book", and that was the first step toward the book you now hold in your hands.

What the Song Book format demonstrates, by looking at one song in depth, is that the song is at the heart of what we love about music. We may be entranced by an entire album or an artist's body of work, but it's that individual song with an indefinable something that catches us and draws us in. Even with the radical evolution of recorded music over the past 100 years, the song has always been the central unit, regardless of whether it's a thick 78-rpm record or a digital file that might never have a physical form. The best songs, or our favourite songs, are like sparkling jewels - from different angles or in different settings, they shine in different ways, but each of them fuses sounds and words into something else entirely distinctive and wonderful.

Some of the chapters in this book are expanded versions of Song Book articles that have appeared in *Shindig!*. Other chapters have been written simply because I was curious about a particular song. All of the songs included in this book were first released between 1964 and 1974, but by no means is this an anthology of "greatest songs of the decade" or "the best song from each year". Think of *Song Book*, the book, as the textual equivalent of crate digging in a record shop. You might recognize some of the songs; you might recognize some of the musicians. You might be interested or turned off, or you might recognize very few or none of them. But, just like every record that you see in a record shop has its own story, each chapter of *Song Book* tells the story of a song. There's a story that the song tells in its lyrics and its music, but there's also a story in how the song itself came to be and where it went. And you may learn something about each song that you didn't know before. Come along on the journey, and listen to these stories.

When You Walk in the Room
Jackie DeShannon
1964

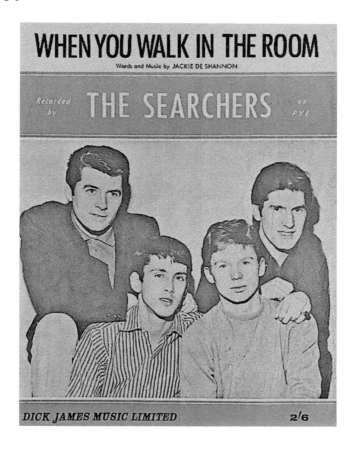

There's two ways that musicians can approach the task of covering a song. One way is to grab the song by the scruff of its neck, toss it around a few times, and then launch it into a completely different dimension. When this strategy works, the results can be stunning transformations: for example, Nazareth's out-of-left-field reinterpretation of Joni Mitchell's 'This Flight Tonight' and Joe Cocker's radical reworking of the Beatles' 'With A Little Help from My Friends'. But when this strategy fails, the results can be awful enough to make grown men and women run away in tears: for example, Britney Spears' attempt at the Rolling Stones' '(I Can't Get No) Satisfaction'. (Thankfully her rumoured cover of Yes' 'I've Seen All Good People' has not been released. Yet.)

The other way to cover a song is for the musicians to respect what made the song great in the first place, and follow the blueprint of the original version. Most of the 60-plus artists who have covered Jackie DeShannon's 'When You Walk in the Room' have done exactly that, and why not? With its chiming harmonies and jaunty guitar riff, the song was power pop perfection before there was even such a thing as power pop. It evokes the inexplicable shivery, giddy thrill of just being near that Special Someone – and adds the wistful twist of being unable to tell that person how you feel about them.

When DeShannon recorded the song herself in mid-'63, she was well established as a songwriter, having written hits for Brenda Lee, Irma Thomas, and the Fleetwoods. But she was still struggling to be recognized as a performer, although she had been singing in public since she was a child. She cycled through several different stage names: first, Sherry Lee Myers, a variation on her real name of Sharon Lee Myers, and then Sherry Lee, Jackie Dee, Jackie Shannon, and Jackie Dee Shannon. She released several unsuccessful singles under these various names, eventually settling on "Jackie DeShannon" as her professional name because she sang in a lower key than most female vocalists, and thus she wanted a gender-neutral first name. Meanwhile, she was also demonstrating remarkably eclectic musical tastes. She performed in a duo with Ry Cooder, and also struck up a friendship with Bob Dylan. "The first time I saw him, his songs made my hair go up like alfalfa," she recalled. DeShannon wanted to record an album of Dylan's songs, but "my record company thought they'd never catch on. I was ahead of the curve, and the world hadn't caught up." She was also constrained by the gender stereotypes of the era that the music industry expected female performers to fit into. "When I began recording songs, if a woman said anything about being a woman she was considered either Debby Dyke or Sally Slut. We weren't supposed to have feelings beyond 'My Boy Lollipop'."

'Needles and Pins', authored by Jack Nitszche and Sonny Bono, was DeShannon's first single to achieve notable commercial success. In addition to the hit solidifying her reputation as a performer, working on the record contributed to building a rewarding professional relationship between DeShannon and Nitszche. "We became very very fast and close friends because we shared the love of so many different styles of music. And he was the arranger for me because I could say anything about, okay, this sounds like this record, and he really knew what I meant." The guitar sound that Nitszche and DeShannon developed for her records has been credited with inspiring the "jangly" guitars of the Byrds and other acts (DeShannon later wrote 'Don't Doubt Yourself Babe' for the Byrds' debut album *Mr. Tambourine Man*, and the Byrds returned the favour by backing DeShannon on her '66 track 'Splendor in the Grass'.)

'When You Walk in the Room' was written by DeShannon while "I was waiting for a date to pick me up — [he] shall remain nameless and has for these many, many years. He doesn't even know that he's the one that I wrote it about. And he was late. And the guitar was sitting there, and I was very excited about the dinner date, and that's how it happened. And I just wrote it pretty fast, actually." Moby Grape's Peter Lewis, who covers the song in his acoustic solo shows, has said that the song was written with Rick Nelson in mind as a potential performer. DeShannon's own version, released in November '63, scraped into the lower reaches of the US Top 100 and made the Canadian Top 30.

Since the Searchers had already had a UK #1 hit with their cover of 'Needles and Pins', it would seem logical to assume that they subsequently decided to record 'When You Walk in the Room' because of that earlier success. Their version of the song marked a significant change for the group because its recording was preceded by the departure of bassist/vocalist Tony Jackson. Thus, 'When You Walk in the Room' was the first Searchers record that featured Jackson's replacement, Frank Allen. Allen has called 'When You Walk in the Room' the best of the Searchers' singles – "it wasn't the biggest hit, but it's the most dynamic. It's the most perfect pop song" - and cites it as the record that best represents his own contribution to the Searchers. "I played the bass on it and also sang a dual lead on it, so that's pretty important for me. For whatever reason we decided to try and give the vocals a different edge by having Mike Pender and myself do the lead in unison, and you can clearly hear my voice on the top."

The Searchers' version of 'When You Walk in the Room', released in '64, became an international hit. While some writers have claimed that DeShannon's own records were then subsequently treated as "mere test pressings for Searchers records", she herself showed no resentment that other artists were having more success with her songs than she was. She told an interviewer in the UK in late '64, "I just feel proud that groups like the Searchers do it. See those red roses over there? They sent them to me..." The Searchers also recorded a version of the song in German; other European acts released Finnish, French, and Italian renditions during the '60s.

The success of 'When You Walk in the Room' partially contributed to DeShannon being chosen as the opening act for the Beatles on their first North American tour in '64. While she appreciated the opportunity to perform on the same bill as the biggest band in the world, she also experienced the fan madness that erupted at every stop of the tour. "I went out the wrong door once, to try to get on the bus to get back to the airplane," she says. "And people were pulling my hair, pulling my clothes. It was really scary. I thought this was going to be it. But they were so crazy, they wanted anyone who had been near [the Beatles]. Anyone that they thought had been close to them -- it was pretty frightening."

The Beatles tour also resulted in DeShannon's version of 'When You Walk in the Room' being released on LP, on a '64 album entitled *Breakin' It Up on the Beatles Tour!*. Despite the album's title, and the cover art featuring an on-stage photo, the album was not a live album from the tour; it was, instead, a compilation of DeShannon's earlier singles. The album's contents also reflected some of her other artistic explorations from that period. Two songs ('She Don't Understand Him Like I Do' and 'Hold Your Head High') were co-written with Randy Newman, himself an emerging songwriter at that time; the album also included DeShannon's rendition of Newman's 'Did He Call Today, Mama?'. Another number, 'The Prince', was co-written with Sharon Sheeley, who DeShannon had previously collaborated with in writing 'Breakaway', a '64 hit for Irma Thomas (and also a hit for Tracey Ullman nearly two decades later).

DeShannon moved to the UK in '65 and worked with Jimmy Page, in addition to writing Marianne Faithfull's biggest hit, 'Come and Stay With Me'. But her most visible successes came soon afterwards, when she returned to the US. Her interpretation of Hal David and Burt Bacharach's 'What the World Needs Now Is Love' charted worldwide in '65, followed in '67 by 'Put A Little Love in Your Heart', which she co-wrote with Jimmy Holiday and her brother Randy. Both songs, released during a time of societal and political turmoil, tapped into a widespread dissatisfaction with the state of the world, and hit a nerve as reminders of the healing power of love and of simply seeing others as fellow humans rather than as enemies. Since then, DeShannon has continued writing and performing, co-authoring Kim Carnes' '81 hit 'Bette Davis Eyes' and revisiting her own back catalogue in 2011 with the largely acoustic album *When You Walk In The Room*, which also shows off her tremendous guitar-playing skills.

The wide-ranging appeal of 'When You Walk in the Room' was demonstrated by its being one of the few non-originals played by Bruce Springsteen and the E Street Band at their legendary summer '75 shows at the Bottom Line in New York City, just prior to the release of *Born to Run*. Allegedly, as a fledgling songwriter, Springsteen and guitarist Steve Van Zandt made a trip to visit DeShannon, who played them unreleased songs she had co-authored with Van Morrison; 'When You Walk in the Room' has been on Springsteen's set lists many times since. The song became a chart hit again in '87 with Paul Carrack's take on it, accompanied by two videos. The UK version featured Carrack as a beleaguered schoolboy tormented by classmates played by the cast of the television sketch show *Who Dares Wins*. Since North American audiences were apparently not capable of appreciating wacky schoolroom hijinks, the US version instead hewed to the standard music-video format of singer-sings-while-model-looks-glamourous.

'When You Walk in the Room' also proved to be one of those rare songs sturdy enough to stand up to interpretations in widely different styles. Both Stephanie Winslow in '81 and Pam Tillis in '94 cracked the US country charts with their versions, with Tillis' accompanied by a delightful video placing her as the star performer in a mid-'60s episode of the *American Bandstand* TV show. Status Quo had a semi-acoustic go at the song on its '96 album *Don't Stop*. Other notable versions came from New Zealand singer Sandy Edmonds in '67, featuring an unusual accelerating sitar-ish opening, and from the vastly underrated Karla Bonoff in '79.

Some interpretations, though, aren't as memorable. Paul Nicholas' '75 version starts with an appealingly slowed-down, tremulous piano-and-vocal introduction, but that initial promise then gets buried under tons of excessively lavish orchestration. The same thing happens with the 2004 version by Agnetha Faltskog (her out of Abba); the demo version of the track posted on YouTube shows how much better a simpler arrangement would have been. And then there's the really-shouldn't-have-bothered electro-pop dance versions by Ramming Speed in '84 and by Dawn Chorus and the Blue Tits (har-har) in '87 – the latter perhaps only notable as an early showbiz venture by future TV presenter Carol Vorderman.

DeShannon told an interviewer in 2009, "I don't want to lose my zip. I always want to be the starry-eyed girl." 'When You Walk in the Room' captures that starry-eyed spirit, and continues to captivate both performers and listeners.

Iko Iko
The Dixie Cups
1964

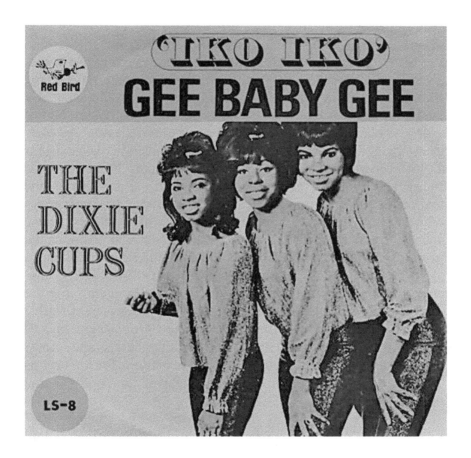

With its rhythmic bounce, repetitive lyrics, and simple melody, 'Iko Iko' sounds like a children's song, and its catchiness has likely enchanted more than a few kids. Indeed, it was Dr. John's two-year-old daughter who chose his rendition of the song to be the single from the *Dr. John's Gumbo* album. However, one thing we learn as adults is that much of the entertainment we loved as children is considerably toned-down versions of violent tales. Young readers might be traumatized by details such as Cinderella's mean stepsisters cutting off their toes to fit their feet into the Prince's glass slipper, and blood pouring from the shoe as they prance around in it. Similarly, 'Iko Iko''s lighthearted feel obscures its origins as a verbal and musical challenge between warring groups in the streets of New Orleans.

There are conflicting versions of who is challenging who in 'Iko Iko'. Further confusion has been added in lyrical variations across the years, as different artists put their own stamp on the song, mishear the words of earlier versions, or try to avoid potentially offensive racial references. One interpretation of the lyrics frames the song as back-and-forth bragging between two krewes, the New Orleans social and cultural societies who are most visible each year with their elaborate themed floats and costumes at Mardi Gras parades. The evidence cited as supporting this possibility is the lyrical mentions of "flags", "green boy" and "red boy", supposedly referencing the distinctive and colourful outfits worn by krewe members. Another slightly more serious interpretation positions the song as a fighting challenge between Native American street gangs vying for reputation and for control over their turf. And yet another interpretation combines the ideas of the first two by identifying the krewes as groups of black Americans adopting the guises of Native American tribes. Given that the history of New Orleans is a history of racial, ethnic, cultural and linguistic interactions and cross-influences, it's possible that all of these explanations for the origins of 'Iko Iko' have some connection to whatever the song's actual sources might be.

The first artist to record the song was James "Sugar Boy" Crawford, in '53, on a single released under the title of 'Jock-a-Mo' and the band name of Sugar Boy and His Cane Cutters. Crawford is also credited as the writer of the song on this release; he told an interviewer in 2009 that he created the song by combining "two Indian chants that I put music to. 'Iko Iko' was like a victory chant that the Indians would shout. 'Jock-A-Mo' was a chant that was called when the Indians went into battle. I just put them together and made a song out of them." He did point out, though, that his original lyric was 'Chock-A-Mo', but Chess Records head Leonard Chess misheard the words and titled the song 'Jock-A-Mo'. When Dr. John recorded the song in '72, the liner notes of his album *Dr. John's Gumbo* explained: "[the song] has a lot of Creole patois in it. Jockamo means 'jester' in the old myth. It is Mardi Gras music, and the Shaweez was one of many Mardi Gras groups who dressed up in far-out Indian costumes and came on as Indian tribes." Researcher Dr. Sybil Kein has suggested that the lyrics are a combination of Creole, the variation of French spoken in the southeastern US, and the African language Yoruba.

The song first found commercial success under the title of 'Iko Iko' with the '65 version by the Dixie Cups. The trio of singers – Barbara Ann Hawkins, her sister Rosa Lee, and their cousin Joan Marie Johnson – were originally from New Orleans, but moved to New York where they were signed to a record deal by producers and songwriters Jerry Leiber and Mike Stoller. Their first hit was 'Chapel of Love' in '64; after a few subsequent and less successful singles, 'Iko Iko' got them back into the Top 20. They told a UK interviewer that they had heard their grandmothers sing the song when they were younger, and while their version is clearly similar to Crawford's, the label of the single credits them as the songwriters. Other sources, probably incorrectly, credit authorship of this version of the song to Ellie Greenwich and Jeff Barry (who co-wrote 'Chapel of Love' with Phil Spector) or to the Dixie Cups' manager, Joe Jones.

Jones may not have written the song, but he certainly seems to have benefited from it, as he was listed as a co-author on several later versions of the song. In 2003, the three members of the Dixie Cups sued Jones, claiming that he owed them unpaid royalties from the song, including their share of licensing fees from when the song appeared on soundtracks of films such as *Mission Impossible II*. The resolution of the lawsuit gave the group members a payment of just over $400,000 US, along with awarding them full control over the song's copyright and distribution. Numerous other New Orleans-based acts, such as the Neville Brothers and the Wild Magnolias, have also recorded or performed the song, and it has become a standard at Mardi Gras time. As it turned out, 'Iko Iko' was the Dixie Cups' last major hit, but their version of the song remains one of the most notable interpretations.

The Dixie Cups' success with the song sparked interest in it by other acts in the '60s. Rolf Harris recorded it in '65, a version that was somewhat overshadowed by the success of 'Jake The Peg', another Harris single from the same year that become one of his signature tunes. The Rockin' Berries also recorded a version in '65. 'Iko Iko' also got considerable traction in translated versions in Europe, with 'Aiko Aiko' from Julie D. in France in '67 and 'Sagamafino' in Italy from the Motowns that same year.

The early '70s saw two distinctively different renditions. In '72, the aforementioned version by Dr. John, which was closer to Sugar Boy Crawford's version than to the Dixie Cups' adaptation, made the US Top 75 as a single. In the same year, Long John Baldry included the song on his album *Everything Stops for Tea* (the title track of which is discussed elsewhere in this book). Baldry's version features a lovely cascading mandolin accompaniment by Davey Johnstone, and enthusiastic backing vocals by producer Elton John. When Baldry performed the song on the *Top of the Pops* TV show, John and Rod Stewart, who were appearing on the same broadcast to promote their own hit singles, decided to liven things up for their old friend by unexpectedly leaping onstage and singing along. The unplanned appearance by the two superstars provoked Baldry - who early in John's career had hired him as a backing musician - to comment to a music journalist after the show, "Who would have thought that this strange boy with his myopic lenses and fat arse could turn out to be one of the pop sensations of all time?" Baldry's 'Iko Iko' was also released in other regions as a single, and improbably became a Top 30 hit in Thailand. International versions also continued elsewhere, with a Finnish 'Aikoo Aikoo' by Jussi and the Boys in '73 and Québecois country singer Patrick Norman's slightly parodic version in '79.

Around '77 the Grateful Dead added 'Iko Iko' to the set lists of their live shows, and the song has since been transported into the repertoires of several of the Dead-related acts that have continued on after the band's formal dissolution in '95. As anyone with even a vague familiarity with the band is aware, the Dead's devoted fans are obsessive chroniclers of practically everything the group ever did. So tracing 'Iko Iko''s history with the band is something that you're welcome to undertake yourself if you have a few months' free time to spare.

In '82, two versions of this song about battles, both by female artists, were battling it out for supremacy on the UK charts. The Belle Stars, a group that evolved out of the 2-Tone act The Bodysnatchers, started their career with a single of 'Iko Iko'. The Belle Stars tend to get lumped in with Bananarama and Amazulu as "those '80s girl groups that happened before the Spice Girls", but, unlike many of their contemporaries, the Belle Stars played all their own instruments and wrote many of their own songs. The group was still finding its feet at the time it recorded 'Iko Iko', and its next two singles were also covers: 'The Clapping Song' and 'Mockingbird'. The more successful '82 UK female version of 'Iko Iko' turned out to be the one by Natasha, whose rendition, with its twangy rubber-bandy bassline, was a Top 10 hit. However, after a subsequent less successful release, Natasha disappeared from the charts, and the Belle Stars had the last laugh by going on to have several top-selling singles with Stiff Records. The Belle Stars' 'Iko Iko' also featured prominently on the soundtrack of the Oscar-winning film *Rain Man*, released that same year. In '82 Tina York covered the song in German as 'Aiko Aiko', and later in the decade Cyndi Lauper made 'Iko Iko' part of her live concerts.

For a song that appeals to children, it's probably inevitable that some actual children and children's entertainers would have a go at it. It would take several pages to list all the kid-friendly acts that have recorded and performed the song, so let's just mention some of those performers that were actually children. Kids Incorporated were one of many acts/TV series in the '80s and '90s featuring singing and dancing pre-teens and barely-teens; they recorded 'Iko Iko' in '89. This version is likely most notable for the presence of cast member Stacy Ferguson, later to become Fergie of the Black Eyed Peas. And then there was 13-year-old Aaron Carter, who melted tweenie hearts with the song on his 2000 album *Aaron's Party (Come Get It)*. For slightly older listeners whose interests had evolved more toward clubbing, there was the Eurodance version by Germany-based Captain Jack in 2001.

A song as well-known as 'Iko Iko' tends to turn up in many contexts, so an overview of 'Iko Iko's' history would be incomplete without mention of a few of its more memorable appearances in pop culture. In '81, the Canadian comedy TV series *SCTV* satirized the film *Chinatown* in its episode "Polynesiantown". Dr. John performed 'Iko Iko' in his role as the house entertainment at a seedy Hawaiian-themed restaurant, in addition to being the sidekick to restaurant owner Johnny LaRue, a.k.a. John Candy. In '88, Justine Bateman and her pals cranked out what was kindly described as an 'inept' version in the marginally successful film *Satisfaction*.

But then 'Iko Iko' became part of possibly one of the most epic cultural crossovers of all time. On April 1 of '93, Barney the Purple Dinosaur – he of annoying 'I Love You, You Love Me' fame – lumbered onto the stage of the Oakland Coliseum to jam on 'Iko Iko' with the Grateful Dead. "Barney" was actually Dead guitarist Phil Lesh, who dressed as the purple monstrosity to play an April Fool's Day prank on his two young sons. Allegedly, when Barney's learned friends heard of their client's unauthorized cameo, they fired off a cease-and-desist letter, and sadly Barney was never seen with the Dead again. (However, his brief shining moment of Deadhead glory is immortalized on YouTube for all to see.)

More recently, in 2016, an all-star jam of a different sort happened on Jimmy Fallon's US TV chat show, when Sia and Natalie Portman joined their host and his house band the Roots for a lively rendition of the song. The Dixie Cups' version of 'Iko Iko' was also prominently featured as a scene-setter in the first episode of the 2017 television adaptation of Neil Gaiman's novel *American Gods*.

The legal saga around the song also continues. In the fall of 2017, a lawsuit alleging unpaid royalties was filed against EMI on behalf of the estate of Dixie Cups member Joan Johnson, who passed away in 2016. The Dixie Cups continue to perform, with Althegra Neville (the Neville Brothers' sister) replacing Johnson, and 'Iko Iko' continues its own longevity, with new versions popping up regularly. Sometimes something simple and catchy turns out to be something enduring.

Morning of My Life/In The Morning
The Bee Gees
1965

It seems that music fans either adore or despise the Bee Gees. The adorers believe that the work of the Gibb brothers has been unjustly ignored, even though it might have been as musically adventurous and innovative as that of the Beatles. The despisers likely feel that they heard more than enough of the Bee Gees during the group's dominance of the disco era. Having lived through the aforementioned era – allegedly, at its peak, at any given moment at least one radio station somewhere in North America was playing a Bee Gees song – I have more than some sympathy for the "enough" argument. But unfortunately the clichés of falsetto vocals and nasty, overly tight polyester trousers have distracted attention from some of the Bee Gees' other, truly lovely music.

'Morning of My Life'– also known as 'In the Morning' – was never a hit, but its brilliance is apparent from the numbers of other artists that have covered it. Using the different times of a single day as connective frames for images of love and companionship, it's sincere and heartfelt, and its melody lends itself equally well to a solo voice or to rich choral and instrumental harmonies.

'Morning' was written by Barry Gibb in '65, while the Gibb family was living in Australia after emigrating from England. Joseph Brennan's wonderfully comprehensive Gibb Songs website indicates that the song was inspired by Donovan's 'Colours'. The Bee Gees – Barry and his twin brothers Maurice and Robin - demoed 'Morning' in the summer of '66 at a small studio in suburban Sydney, during the same recording sessions that produced the hit-to-be 'Spicks and Specks'.

At the time those recordings were made, the Gibb family were already planning to move back to the UK, and it appears that the band's Australian management did not see much value in promoting the careers of performers who were about to move to the other side of the world. Thus, rather than using the demos to promote the Bee Gees themselves, the Gibbs' music publisher instead circulated the demos to attract interest in the songs. That strategy resulted in 'Morning''s first commercial release, as the B-side of a single by pop singer Ronnie Burns. The A-side, 'Exit Stage Right', was also a Barry Gibb composition. John Farrar, who gained later fame through working with the Shadows and Olivia Newton-John, wrote the orchestral arrangement for 'Morning', and his band The Strangers provided the instrumental backing on the single.

In late '66, before the Gibb family set sail for the UK, their father Hugh sent a parcel of the Bee Gees' Australian recordings to Beatles manager Brian Epstein, along with a letter outlining the group's musical achievements. Accounts vary as to whether that parcel included all of the demos from the 'Spicks and Specks' sessions, so it's not clear whether 'Morning' was part of the pitch to Epstein. It's also not clear whether Epstein himself ever actually heard any of the Gibbs' demos. But, fortuitously, fellow Australian Robert Stigwood was alerted that the talented youngsters were about to arrive.

Stigwood had arrived in the UK in '55 as a 21-year-old hitchhiker, and had gradually established himself as a presence in the music industry through his involvement with the success of acts such as John Leyton and Cream. However, in the mid-'60s his companies ran into financial difficulties, which led to Stigwood selling part of his business to Epstein's NEMS organization and becoming NEMS' managing director. He may have heard the Gibbs' demos when they were sent to Epstein; other sources suggest that the Bee Gees' Australian record label notified Stigwood that the Gibb family were moving overseas. Regardless of how Stigwood became aware of the Bee Gees' music, he liked enough of whatever he heard to audition and then sign them after they settled in the UK in early '67.

Stigwood was unsuccessful in making 'Spicks and Specks' a hit in Britain as it had been in Australia, but then he made the Bee Gees stars in the UK with singles such as 'New York Mining Disaster 1941', 'To Love Somebody', and 'Massachusetts'. Barry Gibb described him as "the man who made things happen for us…he believed in us and that elevated us." Meanwhile, Stigwood was apparently also shopping Bee Gees compositions to other artists. The most successful cover of 'Morning' from that period was by Esther and Abi Ofarim in '67. BBC executive Mark Cooper has recalled that the Ofarims' show that year at the Royal Albert Hall was the first "popular music" concert he attended, and that 'Morning' was part of the couple's "undoubted triumph" at a performance that garnered seventeen encores.

Two very different covers of 'Morning' came in '68. Mary Hopkin's crystalline Welsh-language version 'Yn y bore' appeared on her four-song EP *Llais Swynol*, released in May. The sleeve notes described the translated 'Morning' as "bring[ing] the idea of new promise that each dawn presents to everyone". Later that year, Hopkin also performed the original English-language version of the song on a TV special filmed in St. Paul's Cathedral. The other '68 cover was by Nina Simone; you don't need me to tell you that she was a superb interpreter who commandingly transformed other people's songs into her own. Her version of 'In the Morning' was part of the live album '*Nuff Said*; however, that particular track was actually a studio recording with audience noise added in. Simone's upbeat arrangement and dynamic vocal on 'Morning' turned the song into a bracing declaration of self-confidence and positivity.

The pace of the Bee Gees' career slowed somewhat in '69 and '70. Robin Gibb, dissatisfied with Barry's dominance over the group's songwriting, departed to pursue his own solo ventures. During this time, Barry and Maurice Gibb occasionally performed 'Morning' when they made live appearances together; Lulu, then married to Maurice, also recorded 'Morning' at Muscle Shoals Studios in the US for her '70 album *New Routes*.

In mid-'70, Ronnie Burns visited London to see his old friends, and inadvertently nearly caused another misfortune for the group. As recounted by Bee Gees biographer Andrew Môn Hughes, "At his house, Barry took his guest downstairs to show him his gun collection. Handing Ronnie a German Luger, Barry uttered the immortal words 'Careful, it has a hairline trig…' Before Barry could finish what he was saying, the gun went off and its bullet parted his hair, missing him by just millimeters. It seems almost comical now, but at the time it was no laughing matter. 'Barry just went white', Ronnie recalled."

With Barry having survived that incident, and Robin returning to the group, the Bee Gees finally recorded their own version of 'Morning' in September '70. This and several other Bee Gees songs became part of the soundtrack to the '71 film *Melody*, also released under the title *S.W.A.L.K.* The gentle innocence of this slightly slower rendition of 'Morning' perfectly fitted the film's endearing story of young love. The film gained a cult following in the UK and became a major hit in Japan, where the soundtrack album also charted. Around the same time, the original demo of 'Morning' surfaced on *Inception/Nostalgia*, a Bee Gees compilation album briefly released in Europe that is now highly prized by collectors.

It's likely that 'Morning''s appearance on the *Melody* soundtrack gave it wider exposure that inspired another spate of covers. Folksinger Marie Little recorded it on her '71 album *Factory Girl*; jazz vocalist Marian Montgomery (who in '64 had the distinction of releasing the first-ever version of the evergreen 'That's Life') included 'Morning' on her '72 album *Marian in the Morning*. Paper Lace covered 'Morning' in '72 for their second single, prior to their later success with 'Billy Don't Be a Hero' and

'The Night Chicago Died'. Other covers in '72 came from Val Doonican and the German group Love Generation, as well as a considerably up-tempo version by Johnny Mathis on his live-in-Las-Vegas '72 album *In Person*. There was also a reggae interpretation by John Holt in '73.

Since the mid-'70s, covers of 'Morning' have become somewhat less frequent. Andy, the youngest Gibb brother, recorded it in '80 with the intent of including it as a knock-on for his *Greatest Hits* compilation. Although an official music video was released, showing Andy walking pensively along a beach while singing the song, 'Morning' did not make the final version of that album; however, the track has since appeared on other compilations of his work. In '81, German vocalist Mike Telly, also known as Michael Flexig, did a rather bombastic Euro-metal-style cover (think along the lines of 'The Final Countdown'), after which he went on to participate in several of guitarist Uli Jon Roth's musical projects. David Gray has included 'Morning' in his live shows, and in 2010 he performed it with KT Tunstall and Ray LaMontagne on an episode of the BBC television show *Songwriters' Circle*. More recent versions have come from the Dutch vocalists Mathilde Santing in 2006 and Sabrina Starke in 2015.

'Morning' was also frequently part of the Bee Gees' live shows throughout their career. YouTube posters have uploaded several videos of the three Gibbs performing the song at various times; some of them are a little difficult to watch in retrospect because of Maurice's subversive antics, but there's also a gorgeous acoustic rendition from the "One Night Only" Las Vegas concert in '97. Since his brothers' deaths, Barry Gibb has also performed 'Morning' in his solo concerts. The original demo recording of 'Morning' was included on the two Bee Gees compilations titled *Birth of Brilliance* released in '94 and '98 by Festival Records in Australia, and the *Melody* version has been part of several other Bee Gees anthologies.

Most recently, 'Morning''s durability was demonstrated by it being recorded by a second generation of Gibb family musicians. In 2017, the Gibb Collective – consisting of the children of Andy, Barry, Maurice, and Robin – released the album *Please Don't Turn Out the Lights*, with their performances of 10 of their fathers' songs.

Samantha Gibb, Maurice's daughter, coordinated the production, and also contributed a duet of 'Morning' with her brother Adam.

'Morning' is a classic that should transcend any preconceptions about the Bee Gees and their contribution to popular music. It's a sweet song that's charming in its uncomplicated sincerity, and that's something that any music lover should be able to appreciate. If you believe the Bee Gees are underrated geniuses, you don't have to be convinced that 'Morning' is truly enchanting. But if you're still recoiling from Bee Gees disco overload, find 'Morning' and have a listen. It might just change your mind about the quality of music that the Gibbs were capable of creating.

Sunny Goodge Street
Donovan
1965

'Sunny Goodge Street' first saw the light of day on Donovan's second album, *Fairytale* – which, in the fast-paced pop world of the '60s, was also his second album in '65. While other songs on the album such as 'Colours' initially drew more attention, 'Sunny Goodge Street' is perhaps *Fairytale*'s most memorable song. The contrast between its gentle waltzing instrumentation and its hard-edged lyrical urban vignettes was intriguing to listeners – especially those who didn't know there was an actual Goodge Street in London, and thus for whom Goodge Street could have been a mystical passageway in an imaginative Lewis Carroll story.

Fairytale is generally acknowledged as a transitional album in Donovan's career, representing the time when he moved from being the "British answer to Bob Dylan" into developing his own distinctively whimsical style. The album was recorded with only a few backing musicians and minimal instrumentation so as to frame Donovan's acoustic guitar playing and intimate vocals. Donovan speaks of 'Sunny Goodge Street' in particular as an example of how *Fairytale* showed him developing a "new way of seeing" and "moving into another space". He cites Bert Jansch's guitar playing as an influence on the chord structure of the "jazz fusion" song.

'Sunny Goodge Street' is slightly more elaborate than *Fairytale*'s other tracks, anchored by Danny Thompson's droning bowed bass and Skip Alan's steady brushed drums, and the bridge beautifully contrasts the interplay between Harold McNair's flute and Shawn Phillips' electric guitar. But what most listeners remember about 'Sunny Goodge Street' is its powerful imagery: the startling "violent hash smoker" shaking a "chocolate machine", crazed stoners stumbling through "neon streets" and dull "rooms", and a satin and velvet clad magician who Donovan assures us is "Love, Love, Love".

So what, exactly, is the song about? The explanations range from "IT'S ALL ABOUT DRUGS!!!" to it being Donovan's impressionistic experiences as a newcomer to London in the early '60s. Donovan himself has characterized 'Sunny Goodge Street' as being "not just spiritual but [a] bohemian manifestation of change" and "the subculture emerging from the underground and the elusive search for the self". The "DRUGS!!!" interpretation is perhaps not surprising, given that the song has also been described as a "languorous homage to the spot in London's Fitzrovia where the young Donovan would pick up hash." 'Sunny Goodge Street' was likely one of the first pop songs to explicitly mention drugs, with its reference to the "hash smoker" – a reference that allegedly got the song banned from several radio stations. Puzzlingly, the South African Broadcasting Corporation banned two other songs on

Fairytale - 'Candy Man' and 'Ballad of a Crystal Man' – but found 'Sunny Goodge Street' acceptable for airplay.

'Sunny Goodge Street' was released as a single in the US, France and the Netherlands, and on an EP in the UK. It did not reach the charts, but it did not go unnoticed. Soon after *Fairytale* was released, 'Sunny Goodge Street' was recorded by Marianne Faithfull for her '66 album *North Country Maid*. A haunting harmonica wail and graceful guitar support Faithfull's trembling vocals, and it's definitely one of the stronger tracks on one of Faithfull's more overlooked recordings.

'Sunny Goodge Street' also went multi-national. Artist and writer Harrie Geelen translated its lyrics into Dutch, giving it the title 'Draai weer bij' ['Turn Again']. The Dutch-language version was recorded by singer/songwriter Boudewijn de Groot on his self-titled '66 debut album. Like many of the songs on that album, the arrangement closely resembled that of the original; 'Draai weer bij' also appeared on de Groot's *Apocalyps*, a '70 re-release of the '66 album, which, according to de Groot, only differs from the '66 album in that he is wearing a trendy Afghan coat in the cover photo. In '69, a considerably different version of 'Draai weer bij' appeared on Liesbeth List's album *Pastorale*. While this version is at times a little lounge-lizardy, List's appealing vocal and the swinging horn arrangement show that the song can stand up to more than an acoustic-folkie interpretation.

Somewhat more confusingly, in '69 French chanteuse Véronique Sanson released a single entitled 'Le Printemps Est Là'. While Sanson was listed as the song's creator, and the lyrics bore no resemblance to Donovan's words, the melody was similar enough that the song's credits were subsequently modified to name Donovan as the composer.

However, where 'Sunny Goodge Street' likely had the most impact – ironically, for a song whose lyrics were so explicitly situated in the UK – was in North America. In '66, Judy Collins covered the song on her album *In My Life*, which was a groundbreaking album in several ways. It included songs by composers that at the time were relative unknowns (most notably Leonard Cohen and Randy Newman), and it moved away from Collins' earlier simple musical arrangements into a dizzying blend of orchestration and styles that some critics labeled "baroque folk". Collins' interpretation of 'Sunny Goodge Street' – a song that she praised as "like one of those vivid French sort of things" - reels through loopy arpeggios and plucked harps that make the slightly surreal mood of the song even more fantastical.

However, the other North American version of 'Sunny Goodge Street' is the one that should have been huge – the version by Tom Northcott, which seems to be the only version of the song that ever charted as a single anywhere (#20 in Canada in '67). It's recognized as a Canadian pop-psych classic, and Northcott's version may also be the version with the most intriguing back story.

Starting in the early '60s, Northcott was an active singer and musician in the Vancouver music scene - and, unusually for that time, he also ran his own record label, whose releases included several singles of his own compositions. A local DJ who acted as a "finder" for legendary producer Lenny Waronker sent some of Northcott's records to Waronker, who was intrigued enough to sign Northcott to Warner Brothers Records in the United States. Northcott's version of 'Sunny Goodge Street' was recorded in Los Angeles in '67, co-produced by Waronker and Leon Russell, and arranged by Russell. According to Northcott, several members of the famous Wrecking Crew of studio musicians played on the single, including James Burton, Glen Campbell, Larry Knechtel, and Jim Gordon.

Northcott's version of 'Sunny Goodge Street' bears some similarities to Collins' version with its harp arpeggios, but Russell's orchestrations of piccolo trills and lilting, waltzing guitars and harmoniums take the song into psychedelic dreamland. And Northcott's vocal makes the song exceptionally memorable: his strong and powerful tenor is confident, but with a dark and almost desperate tone. (There were actually two versions of the Northcott single, with a "fearless believer" replacing the "hash smoker" on chocolate-machine-shaking duties in the more radio-friendly version.)

In an '88 interview, Northcott described being in San Francisco on the day that his 'Sunny Goodge Street' single was launched in the US – which happened to be a day of the week when *Sgt. Pepper's Lonely Hearts Club Band* was released. He delightedly heard his song becoming the most requested song on San Francisco radio, and he gleefully anticipated the song's popularity spreading across the US and eventually the world. But, gradually, sadly, Northcott watched the record sink out of sight in the wake of the Beatles' masterpiece – his 'Sunny Goodge Street' only barely troubled the US charts at #126. Northcott recorded several other singles with Russell and Waronker, but the only other one to make even a brief appearance on the US charts was his version of Harry Nilsson's '1941'. Warner Brothers never released a complete Northcott album, but Rhino Records' 2012 compilation *Sunny Goodge Street: The Warner Bros. Recordings* includes all of the Warner Brothers singles, in addition to previously unreleased tracks from Northcott's later recording sessions in London with producer Tony Hatch.

In '69, tired of the vagaries of the music industry, Northcott purchased a fishing boat and spent the next 13 years as a commercial fisherman, working the waters of the British Columbia coast. He sold his boat in the early '80s, took a law degree, and embarked on a lengthy career as a lawyer specializing in maritime law and as a respected mediator. He retired from the law in the early 2000s and now lives quietly in southern central British Columbia. Donovan, however, has stayed in the music business and keeps on keeping on. He includes 'Sunny Goodge Street' in his concerts to this day, and while both he and London have changed significantly since the '60s, the song still powerfully evokes the timelessly kaleidoscopic urban experience.

Reason to Believe
Tim Hardin
1966

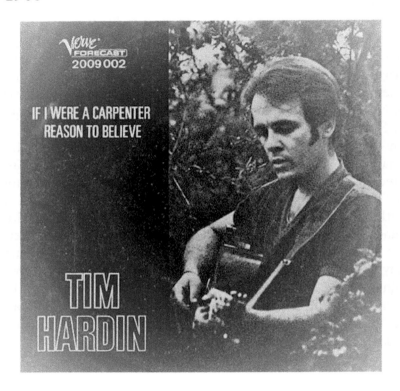

Tim Hardin's song 'Reason to Believe' has a remarkably simple structure, but within that simplicity is a universe of emotional complexity. The lyrics are steeped in the pain of betrayal by a lover, worsened by the inability to stop justifying the lover's deception. Hardin gave very few interviews during his short lifetime, and apparently never spoke specifically about the origins of 'Reason to Believe' – but it is one of the Hardin songs that Charlie Gillett characterizes as "achieving the elusive balance between personal miseries and universal suffering".

'Reason to Believe' was written in '65, and debuted on Hardin's '66 album *Tim Hardin 1*. It was instantly singled out as one of the best tracks on the LP, because Hardin's performance is so deeply affecting. His tremulous vibrato – a vocal style he picked up from listening to jazz singers – adds an extra touch of vulnerability to the poignant lyrics. (He once described his vibrato to an interviewer as "just having [it] in my body, my atoms shake…and I just surrender my body to it".) Hardin claimed that the strings on the album were added without his knowledge or approval, but it can't be denied that Artie Butler's graceful arrangements contribute to the sense of melancholy.

Hardin displayed huge musical potential early in his career, but he also had a turbulent personal life. Born in Oregon, he moved to New York City to attend acting school at the American Academy of Dramatic Art, and then dropped out to become a performer in the folk coffeehouses of New York and Boston. He was signed to a recording contract in '65, but throughout the '60s and '70s he struggled with heroin addiction and substance abuse, and was beset by emotional problems, recurring physical ailments, and broken personal and professional relationships. A series of bad business deals meant that he lost out, by his own estimate, on tens of millions of dollars in royalties – and a considerable portion of that amount probably would have been generated by the numerous covers of 'Reason to Believe'. My searches on the Internet produced references to 86 different versions of the song, from Hardin's in '66 right up to Stephen Stills and Judy Collins' collaboration in 2017.

The first major artist to cover 'Reason to Believe' was Bobby Darin, on his '66 album *If I Were A Carpenter.* Darin started in show business as a songwriter and then had several hits as a performer, with his own songs ('Splish Splash') as well as songs by other composers, such as Kurt Weill and Bertolt Brecht's 'Mack the Knife'. He also was a successful actor, nominated for an Oscar and several Golden Globe awards for his first few film roles; that attention, along with his dark-haired good looks, also led to him becoming a teen idol. But, as might be guessed from the multiple dimensions to his career, Darin was a restless artist: endlessly productive, reluctant to be pigeonholed, and always seeking new sounds and new opportunities.

If I Were A Carpenter was Darin's bid to expand his musical following beyond fans of mainstream pop and nightclub ballads. Some critics dismissed the album as opportunistic folk-rock bandwagon-jumping, especially as Darin's other two album releases that same year were *Bobby Darin Sings 'The Shadow of Your Smile'* and *In A Broadway Bag*. However, others pointed out that in '63 Darin had recorded two albums of traditional and modern folk songs (*Earthy!* and *Golden Folk Hits*), and praised his visionary attention to new styles of music and to the work of newer artists such as Hardin and John Denver. *If I Were A Carpenter* included three Hardin compositions: 'Reason to Believe', the title track (which became a Top 10 hit for Darin in both the US and the UK), and 'Red Balloon', which Hardin himself had recorded but not yet released.

The link between Hardin and Darin was record executive Charles Koppelman, who produced both *If I Were A Carpenter* and Hardin's second album. Several years earlier, Koppelman had pitched a song titled 'Daydream' to Darin – who passed on it, because he had a song of his own that he thought was better. Koppelman gave 'Daydream' to his clients The Lovin' Spoonful, who turned it into their third hit single. After Darin and Koppelman had several more back-and-forths about possible song choices, Darin, by Koppelman's telling, "threw up his hands and said, I'll record whatever song you want me to record." Koppelman then played Hardin's as-yet-unreleased tracks to Darin, and encouraged him to record 'If I Were A Carpenter' and the other two Hardin songs. Hardin reputedly believed that Darin copied not only his vocal style but also the style of the "orchestrated folk-rock" arrangements on Hardin's record. Darin's version of 'Reason To Believe' includes rather startling random bursts of bongo beats, but while there are definite similarities between Hardin's and Darin's renditions of the song, Darin's vocal is sweeter and smoother than Hardin's.

Other artists who covered 'Reason to Believe' in '66 were the duo Just Us, featuring 'Wild Thing' songwriter Chip Taylor and session musician Joe Gorgoni. 'Reason to Believe' was one of several covers on what turned out to be Just Us' only album, but one of the other covers, 'I Can't Grow Peaches on a Cherry Tree', became the single and the hit. Folk/blues singer Karen Dalton also covered the song that year, but her version (captured on a tape of a rehearsal session) was not heard until the 2012 release of the posthumous album *1966*.

Then between '67 and '70 the floodgates opened. In those three years, 'Reason To Believe' was covered by a wide range of artists, in a wide range of styles: easy listening (Andy Williams, the Sandpipers), folk-rock (Ian & Sylvia, Peter, Paul & Mary, Youngbloods, Mason Williams), bluegrass (the Dillards, Hearts & Flowers), country (Nitty Gritty Dirt Band, Glen Campbell), and pop (Jackie deShannon, the Critters, Rick Nelson, David Hemmings). 'Reason to Believe' also was covered in French (as 'Les Choses de l'Amour') by Natacha Snitkine and by Sylvie Patart.

Richard and Karen Carpenter recorded a demo of 'Reason to Believe' sometime between '66 and '68 at bassist Joe Osborn's studio in Los Angeles. The song was part of what were later called "the Magic Lamp sessions", since one of the earliest tracks from those recordings, 'Looking for Love', was released on the small Magic Lamp label. However, the Carpenters didn't release their interpretation of the song until their second album, '70's *Close To You*. 'Reason to Believe' was somewhat overshadowed by the two huge hits from that album, the title track and 'We've Only Just Begun', but Richard Carpenter has said that 'Reason to Believe' is one of his favourites of all of the Carpenters recordings. While the country-flavoured arrangement might seem a little too perky for such a melancholy song, Karen Carpenter's wistful contralto vocal makes the song work. Listening to Karen sing 'Reason to Believe' now, it's hard not to hear it as a foreshadowing of her later struggles with romantic relationships and with her own self-esteem.

Peggy Lee, like Bobby Darin, was a singer who also had success as an actress and a songwriter. By the mid-'60s, she was largely perceived by her label Capitol Records as being past her prime - but a young producer, Karl Engemann, was inspired by Darin's career revitalization with 'If I Were A Carpenter'. He brought in Charles Koppelman and his producing partner, Don Rubin, to work with Lee. Koppelman and Rubin encouraged Lee to record 'Reason to Believe' in March '68, along with a second Hardin song, 'Misty Roses', and The Lovin' Spoonful's 'Money'. Recording 'Reason to

Believe' was a challenge for Lee, as the session marked the first time she had sung to a pre-recorded arrangement instead of performing live in the studio with a backing band. Nevertheless, Lee liked 'Reason to Believe' and "connected with its angry words", and its unusual arrangement by Shorty Rogers, featuring a funked-up bass line, certainly distinguished Lee's version from other covers of the song.

However, perhaps wanting to hedge their bets on Lee's new artistic direction, Capitol executives also persuaded Koppelman and Rubin to record an album of Lee in concert. This resulted in the taping of two of Lee's performances at the Copacabana in New York City in April '68, including her live version of 'Reason to Believe'. Shortly afterwards, Lee's studio version of the song was released as a single, backed by her cover of The Lovin' Spoonful's 'Didn't Want to Have to Do It'. The single flopped, and the live album, titled *2 Shows Nightly*, was withdrawn soon after its release, allegedly because Lee was dissatisfied with the quality of the recording and mixing. (It's since been re-released on CD.)

In '69, soul singer Maxine Brown covered 'Reason to Believe' on her album *We'll Cry Together*; the daringly slow arrangement sounds like it shouldn't work, but it does – and Brown's passionate vocal makes this one of the more memorable versions of the song. But then in '71, Rod Stewart released what is probably the best-known cover of 'Reason to Believe', on his album *Every Picture Tells A Story*. Before Stewart's career veered into disco, supermodels, and desecrations of the Great American Songbook, he was regarded as a discerning musical connoisseur with an unerringly accurate ear for good songs. In the words of journalist John Pidgeon, "You didn't become as successful as Rod did by being a tosser, and he wasn't one". With an arrangement driven by Pete Sears' piano and Ian McLagan's Hammond organ, and embellished by Dick Powell's jazzy violin licks, Stewart takes some vocal liberties with Hardin's straightforward melody, but convincingly conveys the song's weariness and resignation.

'Reason to Believe' was the A-side of the first single from *Every Picture Tells A Story*, and reached #62 in the US charts and #19 in the UK charts. But then radio DJs started turning the single over and playing the B-side, 'Maggie May'. The response to that song was so immediate and strong that the single was reissued with 'Maggie May' as the new A-side. 'Maggie May' went on to become Stewart's first worldwide #1 single and one of his most successful records ever. However, 'Reason to Believe' is still one of Stewart's signature songs, included in almost every anthology of his work and in his live shows. In '93, Stewart performed the song in his *Unplugged...And Seated* MTV television special, accompanied by Ronnie Wood on acoustic guitar. The single of the MTV performance went to #19 on the US charts, giving Stewart the rare distinction of having two hits 20 years apart with the same song.

The success of Stewart's 'Reason to Believe' generated new interest in the song. In subsequent years, it has been recorded by, among others, Cher, Lynn Anderson, Skeeter Davis, Jerry Vale, Johnny Cash, Billy Bragg, Vonda Shepherd, Ron Sexsmith, and Wilson Phillips – a list of artists that probably have absolutely nothing else in common. 'Reason to Believe' also made its way into the live sets of Crosby Stills & Nash, John Denver, John Stewart, Jesse Colin Young, Barry McGuire, Cliff Richard, Kim Carnes, and the Jayhawks. But astoundingly, despite Hardin's tragic death at age 39 in '80, it took until 2013 for a Hardin tribute album to be released – and it speaks to the reputation of 'Reason to Believe' that the song's title was also chosen as the title of the album. The Sand Band from Liverpool were given the honour of covering 'Reason to Believe' on the tribute album; their low-key rendition, with mournful steel guitar and harmonica, is movingly sincere. The album contains many other excellent renditions of Hardin songs, including Mark Lanegan's 'Red Balloon', the late Gavin Clark's 'Shiloh Town', and Okkervil River's 'It'll Never Happen Again'. That songs from several decades ago can sound so contemporary and can appeal to an entirely new audience is a testament to Hardin's enormous talent and to the lasting impact of his work.

A Place in the Sun
Stevie Wonder
1966

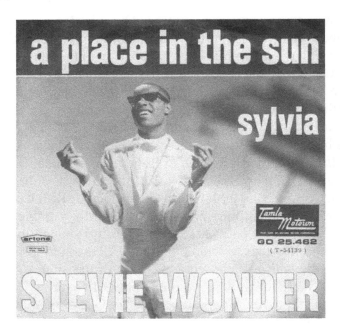

Motown Records started in 1960, which in retrospect is appropriate because of Motown's incredible influence on the '60s – not only its influence on music, but also its influence on society as a highly successful company created and operated by black Americans. Despite Motown's achievements, however, by the mid-'60s there were indications that Motown was starting to head into turbulent waters. The music industry was shifting away from the model of producers and executives exerting tight control over artists – a model which Motown excelled at – towards a model that put artists in charge of their own music. Some Motown staff questioned whether the company was capable of adapting to that shift; there were also rumblings of discontent from several Motown artists and songwriters about the perceived unfairness of their contracts.

Although Motown was one of the top record companies in the US and its artists were recognized around the world, Berry Gordy, Motown's founder and president, wanted to expand the company's presence beyond the music industry and for it to become a producer of television shows and films. As a result, he was spending more time in Los Angeles than he was at Motown's Detroit headquarters. Many at Motown felt that the company was suffering because of Gordy's absences and because of his ambitions, which they thought were taking Motown too far away from its musical expertise. Gordy was also being criticized for his relative public silence on the racial inequality that was starting to boil over in many parts of the United States – which, for Motown, was not an abstract issue. Among other things, many Motown artists were regularly subjected to racist threats or attacks while on tour, and Motown representatives experienced discrimination from other parts of the record industry such as radio stations and record stores. Several Motown acts were also expressing frustration at the company's focus on entertainment rather than on social commentary.

But amongst that mess of uncertainty came 'A Place in the Sun', a song that spoke profoundly both of struggle and of hope for a better world. It was first recorded in '66, and by '70 nearly 20 artists had covered it, which indicates how relevant it was to the troubled times inside and outside Motown.

Ron Miller and Bryan Wells, the song's co-authors, were unlike the majority of Motown's staff songwriters in that both were white. Both also came to Motown through quirks of serendipity. One version of the story of Miller's discovery was that, as an aspiring songwriter, he was delivering pizzas to pay the bills, and happened to bring an order to Motown staff writer Mickey Stevenson, with the result that Stevenson set up a meeting between Miller and Gordy. The other version was that Gordy discovered Miller performing in a Detroit bar. However the two got together, though, their first formal meeting was memorable. In his autobiography, Gordy recounted that the first thing Miller said to him in his Motown office was, "Mr. Gordy, I don't want to write that Blues shit." Rather than being offended, Gordy instead recognized the potential in a songwriter whose tastes ran to Broadway musicals; Gordy even set up a separate music publishing company, Stein and Van Stock, to give the impression that Miller's new compositions were little-known "old classics".

Miller's first few songs for Motown were given to Marvin Gaye, who, as a fan of singers such as Nat King Cole, had a soft spot for crooners and ballads. Two Miller compositions were on Gaye's '64 album *Hello Broadway*, and Miller's 'My Way' became the single from that album. Both were flops, but, according to Gordy, Miller blamed the failure on "the public's poor taste". Gordy told him, "You can worship your own stuff in your basement for the rest of your life, or you can try to write something a million people can relate to." Miller "got the point" and started churning out hits such as 'For Once in My Life'.

Wells met Miller in May '66, when, as a college student, he was playing an unexpected gig at a piano bar. "I was subbing for one of my agent's other clients, and I was cramming for finals at the time so I didn't really want to do it." Miller, "a handsome devil", approached Wells and asked if he had written anything himself. "So I played one, and then he told me who he was and that he was looking for someone to work with. And that's how it started."

In his songwriting partnership with Miller, says Wells, "there was a clear division of labour. I wrote the music first and then presented him with the melodies. And because we were both consummate professionals, it was impossible for him to write junk." Some sources claim that 'A Place in the Sun' was inspired by the '25 book of the same name and its '51 film adaptation, but Wells denies that - although, he says, he and Miller were glad to find out "that you can't copyright a title."

The song brought something different to Motown because, in Wells' words, "it's more of a country tune. Not like Faith Hill and Tim McGraw, but the melody and the chord structure are like traditional country." Wells and Miller wrote the song with Stevie Wonder in mind. At that point in his career, Wonder had already had two #1 singles but was maturing past his "boy genius" phase and trying new creative possibilities. As a young black man, he was also mindful of the social upheavals which Motown executives seemed determined to ignore.

Clarence Paul, Wonder's producer, seized upon the demo of 'A Place in the Sun' and recorded a version of it himself. Paul then took his version to one of Motown's legendary "Friday meetings". At these "quality control" sessions, producers and songwriters presented potential releases for critique and feedback, and argued their case for why a song should be a single or should be given to a particular artist. Gordy has said that everyone at these meetings was on "equal ground" and was free to speak their mind and challenge others' opinions, including his own. Wells never attended the Friday meetings – "those were for the executives and producers, I was too far down the totem pole" – but when Paul played his own version of 'A Place in the Sun' to the Friday group, Gordy's response was, "No, this is for Stevie."

'A Place in the Sun' debuted on Wonder's '66 album *Down to Earth*. The cover photo of the album made it plain that this marked a new direction for Wonder; rather than depicting him dressed up and on stage, he was shown in everyday clothes, playing his harmonica on grimy, graffiti-marked outdoor steps. 'A Place in the Sun' became the album's single, and, Wells recalls, "it really was a change from his earlier songs like 'Fingertips'. And for some people, that was too much of a departure. I remember the first time I heard it played on the radio, right after it finished there was a call-in. It was a teenage girl, and she said 'Oh, I don't like that *at all*'. And I thought, 'Well, I'm doomed'." Thankfully, that listener's opinion was not widely shared, as the song charted in the US in '66 and in the UK in '67.

Just after *Down To Earth* was released, Gordy decided to create a collaboration between two of Motown's best-selling acts, the Supremes and the Temptations. The collaboration was an example of Motown's strategy of "piggybacking" – putting two groups together to broaden each one's audience. The hip, about-to-be-psychedelic Temptations could bring younger, cooler listeners into The Supremes' older supper-club-and-Vegas audience, and vice versa. However, many Motown insiders suspected that Gordy's real motive in teaming the two acts was to create another showcase for his girlfriend Diana Ross – especially since the collaboration was announced not long after The Supremes had officially become "Diana Ross and The Supremes". Another reason for the suspicion was that the pairing was musically problematic. When the two groups sang together, Ross' "thin, wispy zephyr of a voice" was overwhelmed by the "bellows" of Temptations lead singer David Ruffin. The other Supremes and Temptations, most of whom had known each other since childhood, were also not particularly happy at being ordered to address the budding solo star as "Miss Ross".

The situation worsened when the two groups clashed during preparations for their first joint television appearance, on the *Ed Sullivan Show* in the summer of '67. On the first day of rehearsals, it became apparent that the two groups were used to singing in different keys - and while Ruffin and the Temptations could easily sing in the keys the Supremes used, Ross struggled to sing in the keys of the Temptations' arrangements. The next day, when the groups came back into the rehearsal studio, the charts for the backing musicians had been rewritten so that all the songs were in Ross' preferred keys. According to Tony Turner, who worked as a Motown road manager, the Temptations were shocked at the unexplained change, and were even more shocked when the other two Supremes told them that Ross "did this all the time" and that Ross considered the Temptations to be "riding on her coattails".

Despite the increasing tension and hostility, the two groups began work on a joint Supremes/Temptations album in early '68, and 'A Place in the Sun' was chosen as one of the album's tracks. In June, the album's progress was delayed when the Temptations decided they had had enough of dealing with Ruffin's ego and his substance abuse problems, and fired him. Dennis Edwards, a long-time friend of the group, was quickly hired as Ruffin's replacement, but the change meant that Edwards had to re-record Ruffin's vocals on the tracks that had already been completed. *Diana Ross & The Supremes Join The Temptations* was finally released in November '68, with Ross getting top billing and being prominently featured in the centre of the album's cover art. The Supremes/Temptations' take on 'A Place in the Sun' suffers somewhat from not sounding entirely unified – it's more like the two groups are taking turns at singing the song – but the vocal harmonies throughout are stunning.

'A Place in the Sun' was also covered in '67 and in '68 by many different acts: Sandy Posey, Engelbert Humperdinck, the New Christy Minstrels, the Four Tops, the Flames, David Isaacs, and the

Staple Singers. Wells cites the versions by Glen Campbell (on '68's *A New Place in the Sun*) and the Young Rascals as particular favourites. "The Young Rascals did an eight-minute-long version, it was an astonishing epic. And it was the only song on their record ['67's *Groovin'*] that wasn't an original. That was a great tribute." The song has subsequently been recorded by, among others, the Family Dogg, the Persuasions, and Billy Eckstine.

Wells and Miller went on to write two more hits for Wonder: 'Yester-Me, Yester-You, Yesterday' and 'Someday at Christmas'. Miller also wrote 'Heaven Help Us All' for Wonder, and co-authored Ross' '73 hit 'Touch Me in the Morning'. He then worked as a producer for Motown artist Charlene, and co-wrote her single 'I've Never Been to Me', which went largely unnoticed when it was originally released in '77 but became an unexpected worldwide hit when it was re-released in '82. Miller passed away in 2007; Wells went on to become a composer of music for commercials and television shows, and is now a jazz pianist in New York, where he "holds court" as a performer at the Palm restaurant in Manhattan. It's a tribute to the timelessness of 'A Place in the Sun' that, 50 years after it was composed, Wells still gets requests for it. "People will ask for it and I'll play it. I'm not a vocalist, but there's the delight of hearing the interpretation."

Wasn't It You
Goffin & King/Petula Clark
1966

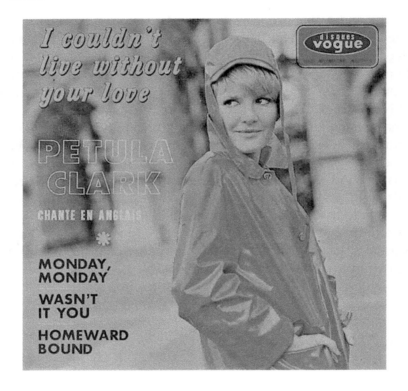

Great songs often come from imagination and from personal experience. The best songwriters are alchemists who can mix ingredients from both of those sources and create something unique. If a song contains an element of imagination, what's going on in that song may not always reflect what's really going on in the songwriter's own life. But in the case of Gerry Goffin and Carole King, it's entirely possible that the tension in their personal relationship sparked their '66 composition 'Wasn't It You'.

King got started in the music business by playing on demo recordings of other acts' songs, along with her friend Paul Simon, when she was a young college student. But while at college she met Goffin, and started writing songs with him. She admired "his ability, in really simple words, big ideas, big feelings, big thoughts - to get inside a woman's head and say the things a woman was thinking." The 20-year-old Goffin and the 17-year-old King hastily married in '59, when she unexpectedly became pregnant. But that same year they were signed to the Aldon music publishing house run by Al Nevins and Don Kirshner, and, starting with the Shirelles' 'Will You Love Me Tomorrow' in '60, they established themselves as a highly successful songwriting team.

By the end of '65, over 50 artists had recorded Goffin & King songs, with more than a dozen of those records becoming Top 20 hits in the US, the UK, or both. John Lennon once said that as young musicians he and Paul McCartney wanted to be the "Goffin-King of England". Goffin also co-wrote hits with Barry Mann ('Who Put the Bomp') and Jack Keller ('Run to Him'), and as a singer King had a US and UK hit in '62, with her and Goffin's 'It Might As Well Rain Until September'.

The couple became the parents of two young daughters, and earned enough money to live comfortably in suburban New Jersey, in a house with a doorbell that chimed the first few notes of 'Will You Love Me Tomorrow'. They were lauded by their peers and by the musicians that played their songs, celebrated for the brilliance of their lyrics and their creative arrangements. But both Goffin and King became restless. King felt trapped by the expectations of the traditional roles of mother and housewife, and Goffin, inspired by Bob Dylan, wanted to explore life beyond pop songs and fatherhood.

Upheavals in American society – the civil rights movement, feminism, anti-war protests – and the changes in popular music personified by artists like Jimi Hendrix motivated Goffin and King to explore new artistic directions. But their songwriting accomplishments also pigeonholed them as just another part of the staid, superficial music industry that newer acts were rebelling against. King biographer Sheila Weller suggested that "[t]he idealist euphoric energy that massed around Dylan and the Beatles was something that Gerry and Carole felt part of, but that their music didn't match."

In '65, the entrepreneurial Goffin and King started their own record company, Tomorrow Records, in partnership with journalist Al Aronowitz. Tomorrow's first signing was the Myddle Class, a five-piece New Jersey rock band who seemed to be a group with potential. However, much to King's distress, Aronowitz introduced Goffin to LSD, which, along with Goffin's "prodigious" use of other substances, sent him into a mental health crisis. Goffin spent time in a psychiatric hospital and underwent shock therapy, and, King, in her own words, "sought relief by going to clubs, concerts, and other activities more appropriate for a young single woman." Through going to watch the Myddle Class play in New York City clubs, King was introduced to a range of artists and musicians that included James Taylor and future members of the Fugs.

Not surprisingly, given that turbulent environment, many of Goffin and King's '66 compositions – 'Don't Bring Me Down', 'Goin' Back', 'Yours Until Tomorrow' – alluded to dissatisfaction, and 'Wasn't It You' followed a similar direction. Goffin's lyrics taunted someone who once claimed that "life's a holiday", but was now "feeling down" after their "gypsy friends" deserted them to entertain someone else. King's musical framework of minor chords and a surging melody contributed to the sense of abandonment and disillusion.

'Wasn't It You' was never recorded by its composers, and was never a hit. But the number of times that it's been covered suggests that musicians and producers recognized that it's a great song, particularly for strong female voices. So it was fitting that Petula Clark did the first cover version of the song, released in the UK in the same year the song was written.

Clark herself was going through an artistic transition in '66. *I Couldn't Live Without Your Love,* the album that included 'Wasn't It You', was her first album to feature songs from writers other than Tony Hatch, her long-time producer. Despite the hyper-romantic title, the album featured a number of songs with a cynical take on romance, and Clark's precise diction and robust vocals give a particular edge to 'Wasn't It You'. *I Couldn't Live Without Your*

Love reached #11 on the album charts and remains Clark's highest-charting album in the UK.

Billie Davis – "a performer, a craftswoman" according to Simon Frith – released 'Wasn't It You' as a single in '67. Davis was one of manager/producer Robert Stigwood's first clients and was widely recognized as a highly distinctive and skilful singer, but was sadly unable to make a commercial breakthrough. 'Wasn't It You' was a fabulous fit for what Tom Hibbert described as Davis' "beautifully controlled, shivery voice", but the single failed to make any serious impression. Spanky and Our Gang, the US group led by singer Elaine 'Spanky' McFarlane, also recorded 'Wasn't It You' in '67, as part of a live album, although the album itself was not released until '70.

The Action were including 'Wasn't It You' in their live act as early as mid-'66, a transitional time in the band's career. An initially promising relationship with Beatles producer George Martin had fallen apart after the failure of several Martin-produced singles, and the band was moving from its mod roots to a "love of the American West Coast sound" and jazz-influenced instrumentals. A *Melody Make*r review of a September '66 gig described the Action's performance of 'Wasn't It You' as "well-arranged [and] smartly executed". However, their dynamic interpretation of the song was not released on record until '68, and then only as the B-side to a German single of 'Harlem Shuffle'. Since then, though, it has been anthologized several times, and has also inspired covers by more recent mod-influenced acts such as the Harries, the Laynes, and Groovy Cellar.

Three other '68 versions of 'Wasn't It You' are all connected in different ways to producer/manager Lou Adler. Canadian folk-pop group 3's A Crowd, the first act to record songs by Bruce Cockburn and Murray McLauchlan, performed 'Wasn't It You' as part of their live shows, and then recorded 'Wasn't It You' for their sole album, *Christopher's Movie Matinee*. According to group member Brent Titcomb, 3's A Crowd were signed to Adler's Dunhill Records "after The Mamas and The Papas had broken up, and we were seen as a similar type of act that could fill that spot in Dunhill's roster." *Christopher's Movie Matinee* was co-produced by Cass Elliot, also managed by Adler, and she sang backing vocals on 'Wasn't It You'.

The combination of her vocal harmonies with those of lead singer Donna Warner make this one of the more appealing versions of the song.

Australian singer Lynne Randell – "Australia's Miss Mod" - had several hits in her home country and then relocated to the US, where she scored the opening spot on a '67 tour featuring Hendrix and Adler's clients the Monkees. Her '68 version of 'Wasn't It You' was her third US single, but like the others it went largely unnoticed, despite Randell's dramatic vocal and the groovy organ-driven arrangement.

Adler produced actress Peggy Lipton's self-titled album in '68, which included 'Wasn't It You' along with several of Lipton's own compositions and two other Goffin/King songs ('[You Make Me Feel Like A] Natural Woman' and 'It Might As Well Rain Until September'). At the time the record was made, Lipton was something of an 'It Girl' in the US because of her starring role as the fashionable undercover policewoman Julie Barnes on the popular TV show *The Mod Squad*. She was also Adler's girlfriend, which meant that her album received "star treatment", including instrumental backing by "the cream of Hollywood session musicians". Unlike most of the female singers who covered 'Wasn't It You', Lipton had a soft, gentle voice; one reviewer stated, "Lipton's rather wispy voice isn't outstanding, [but] neither is it unpleasant." Her singing style doesn't doom her interpretation of the song, but unfortunately her vocals are often overwhelmed by the loud and elaborate instrumentation.

Oddly, covers of 'Wasn't It You' featuring male vocalists are relatively rare. Hamilton Streetcar, a band initially produced by Lee Hazlewood, released their lone album on Dot Records in '69. Their 'Wasn't It You' sounds heavily Doors-influenced, with Ralph Plummer's deep vocal reverberating atop ominous keyboard chords and piercing guitars. Another Hazlewood-affiliated act, the Kitchen Cinq - led by singer/guitarist Mark Creamer - recorded 'Wasn't It You' sometime in the late '60s, but this brassy interpretation remained unreleased until Light in the Attic's 2012 anthology *When the Rainbow Disappears*. And in '91, Norwich's Goober Patrol thrashed and shouted their way through an unlikely punked-up version.

Goffin and King's marriage ended in '68, as did their professional relationship – after enduring the demise of their marriage, King said, "I was too upset to write with him." However, they later resumed their collaboration, creating the song 'Smackwater Jack' for King's '71 album *Tapestry*, which is still one of the best-selling albums of all time. Goffin also worked with other co-writers on hits such as Gladys Knight and the Pips' 'I've Got To Use My Imagination' and Whitney Houston's 'Saving All My Love For You'. But Goffin and King's musical collaborations from the first half of the '60s have endured as classics of modern pop and rock songwriting – as demonstrated by the success of the 2013 musical *Beautiful,* based on King's life story and featuring many of her and Goffin's songs. While 'Wasn't It You' may have initially reflected Goffin and King's own personal conflicts, its sharp depiction of painful rejection resounded with much wider audiences. It may be one of the lesser-known songs in the Goffin/King canon, but it is a gem in that very rich treasury.

The First Cut is the Deepest
Cat Stevens/P.P. Arnold
1967

'The First Cut is the Deepest' has been a hit for several artists in several countries over several decades, but's it a challenging song to unravel. Its composer, Cat Stevens, has said, "The words of my songs speak for themselves", and many of the artists who have covered the song don't appear to have much to say about it either. But a performance of 'The First Cut is the Deepest' has often marked a time of transition in an artist's career – the ideal time for a song about moving into a new relationship while still dealing with the emotional baggage of a previous relationship.

Cat Stevens, the former Steven Georgiou, may have recorded a demo of 'First Cut' as early as '65, and it was likely among the dozen or so songs that he played at his '66 audition for producer Mike Hurst. As the son of a Greek restaurateur and a Swedish mother, a pupil at a Catholic school, and a child growing up in London's lively, multicultural West End, Stevens absorbed an eclectic range of influences that bubbled up into the "lyrical eccentricity" of his first attempts at songwriting. Through his older sister's record collection, he was introduced to the music of George Gershwin, Frank Sinatra and Nat King Cole; he also became enamoured with Buddy Holly and Little Richard, as well as Bob Dylan, the Beatles, and Broadway musicals.

A self-described awkward introvert, Stevens turned to music and art as his means of self-expression, beginning with "one-fingered playing" on the piano in his father's restaurant, the Moulin Rouge on Shaftesbury Avenue. He also studied drawing in school. After Stevens turned 15, his father bought him an acoustic guitar, and he became involved in the folk music scene centered around the Les Cousins club in Soho – although he admits that usually "I was too shy to play more than one or two songs."

Hurst liked what he heard at Stevens' audition, and signed him to the Deram record label. Stevens quickly adopted his new name - "I needed a name people wouldn't forget; my songs weren't particularly commercial but I was very commercially minded" – and started making records. He quickly found success with the '66 singles 'I Love My Dog' and 'Matthew and Son', and then, to his dismay, discovered that success created the expectation of more success. He told interviewer Michael Wale, "It's not as easy as that because the songs aren't like that. Life isn't like that, you just don't do the same thing over and over again. You do it another way, somewhere else."

In early '67, Hurst was also working with vocalist P.P. Arnold, an American soul singer who had come to the UK while touring as an Ikette in the Ike & Tina Turner Revue. After being encouraged by Mick Jagger to pursue a solo career, she quit the tour to stay and work in the UK. She was signed to Andrew Loog Oldham's Immediate label, but after the failure of her first single 'Everything's Gonna Be Alright', Hurst went in search of new material for her. Stevens "had this song and it wasn't finished, but the idea was there, the title and everything and the basic tune. Pat [P.P.] needed a song, so I played a few things and we just finished this one. It really suited her, but I can't say I wrote it for her because I can't do that sort of thing." Arnold told the BBC years later that the lyrics of 'First Cut' resonated with her because they reminded her of the "very abusive teen marriage" she had escaped from. Her stormingly soulful rendition, released in May '67, was framed by Hurst's unusual arrangement using "double everything" – two drums, two basses, and two string sections - and a harp plucking out the song's catchy riff. Hurst said he "loved every moment" of making the record.

The single received mixed reviews; *Record Mirror*'s Peter Jones stated, "It starts rather delicately, with off-beat backing sounds... Then builds into a typical Immediate burst of sound. The beat accentuated and PP fairly roars through this excellent song. I like it — but confess you may have to listen a couple of times before flipping." Nevertheless, Arnold's 'First Cut' became popular enough to reach #18 on the UK charts – but while the hit built Stevens' reputation, it didn't build his bank account; he allegedly received a mere £30 for letting Arnold record his song.

In October '67, Stevens recorded 'The First Cut is the Deepest' himself, for his second album *New Masters* which was released in December of that year. By that time, the relationship between Stevens and Hurst had deteriorated to the point where, according to Hurst, "[w]e did the album with lawyers actually in the studio. It was horrendous." When asked to compare his take on the song to Arnold's, Stevens said, "I didn't like my version too much. I preferred hers." In mid-'68, a bout with tuberculosis, exacerbated by stress and overwork, put Stevens in the hospital for several months. During that time, he rethought his musical direction, and re-emerged as the bearded troubadour who became an international star with albums such as *Mona Bone Jakon* and *Tea for the Tillerman*. (Stevens was also able to use his art school training in creating these albums, by drawing the pictures for the covers.)

'First Cut' also made a detour to Jamaica in '67. At his renowed Studio One, Sir Coxsone Dodd produced Norma Fraser's reggae version of the song, which was released in October on a double single with Bumps Oakley's 'Rag Doll'. Back in the UK, in '68, the Koobas took the song in another direction with their fuzztone- and echo-drenched interpretation, laced with searing guitar solos.

As a DJ on Radio Caroline, Keith Hampshire likely would have been familiar with both Arnold's and Stevens' 'First Cut'. During his stint at the pirate radio station, Hampshire released a novelty single under the name of "Keefers", but it was only after the UK-born Hampshire returned to his home in Canada that he seriously pursued a recording career. Hampshire's '73 rendition of 'First Cut' - produced by Bill Misener, a former member of Toronto psych legends The Paupers - was a #1 hit in Canada and made the Top 10 in Australia. Its horn-powered arrangement evoked the sound of other popular bands of the time such as Lighthouse and Blood, Sweat and Tears; indeed, more than a few commentators noted the vocal similarities between Hampshire and BST's David Clayton-Thomas.

Dozens of covers of the song followed in subsequent years, including numerous reggae interpretations by such well-known acts as Marcia Griffiths, Judy Mowatt, Dawn Penn, and I-Roy. But many of the non-reggae versions, unfortunately, demonstrated how hard it is to perform this song well. 'First Cut' has a gorgeous melody and chord progression – highlighted in Martin Simpson's charming slide-guitar instrumental interpretation - but to truly capture its lyrical dimensions, a singer must convey vulnerability, world-weariness, *and* determination. The two versions of 'First Cut' that were most successful in the US are examples of when this is and isn't accomplished.

Rod Stewart recorded 'First Cut' during the sessions for his '75 album *Atlantic Crossing*, after his move to the US. Producer Tom Dowd cut the track with Stewart and the legendary house band at Muscle Shoals studios. Dowd recounted how, on their first visit, "I introduced Rod to Barry Beckett, Roger Hawkins, Jimmy Johnson and so on, and Rod just looked and took me by the arm, walked me back out of the door, and said, 'That's not the Muscle Shoals Rhythm Section, they're all white'. In his mind, that rhythm section had to be all black. And I said 'Rod, that is them.' And he still said he didn't believe it, and he was being adamant. So I said 'All right', and I went inside and said 'Fellas, here are the chords, key of C, run it down at about this tempo', and they started doing it. Rod was still standing outside the door, and he looked in and said, 'I don't believe it. They're black, but they're all white'!" Stewart's version of 'First Cut' wasn't released, however, until it appeared on his '76 album *A Night on the Town*.

The appalling 'Tonight's the Night' was the first single from that uneven album, but 'First Cut' was roundly praised by reviewers. Bud Scoppa in *Phonograph Record* noted, "[It] has all the poignance and passion of the mature Rod Stewart. When he hits the chorus — 'When it comes to being lucky she's cursed/ When it comes to loving me she's worse' — there's no doubt that Stewart owns those lines absolutely." Even the usually surly Lester Bangs grudgingly admitted, "I would never have believed *anyone* could make Cat Stevens palatable, much less this moving, for me." 'First Cut' eventually became the third single from *A Night on the Town*. Released in '77, it reached #19 in the US and #1 in the UK, where, in a temporary victory for spandex and eyeliner, it kept the Sex Pistols' 'God Save The Queen' from topping the singles charts.

Sheryl Crow's 2003 interpretation of 'First Cut' was initially released as an album-only track on her greatest-hits compilation *The Very Best of Sheryl Crow*, but it received so much airplay that it was released as a single. She has attributed her choice of 'First Cut' as a song to cover to her "strong sense of melancholy". Crow is an enormously accomplished musician who often doesn't get the credit she deserves for the quality of her work, but her take on 'First Cut' is overly glossy and emotionally monotone. This could be one of those records where a highly stylish video has more to do with a record's success than does the song itself. Nevertheless, Crow's 'First Cut' became a crossover hit by reaching #14 in the US pop charts and #35 in the US country charts, thus paving the way for Crow's current career direction as a country artist.

In '77, after a near-death experience, Stevens became a Muslim and changed his name to Yusuf Islam. He abandoned his musical career and, according to several reports, went through his song catalogue to identify songs he deemed as being "anti-God" and which he then disassociated himself from. It's not clear whether 'First Cut' was ever on that list, but it seems unlikely that it was, because when Yusuf returned to live performing in the early 2000s,

'First Cut' was part of his shows – and he still plays it now, as do Crow and Stewart. In his autobiography, Stewart noted that the song "has been enormously good to me over the years". And when P.P. Arnold returned to live performing in 2017 to support the release of her album *The Turning Tide* (recorded in the mid-'60s but tied up in contractual shenanigans until now), 'First Cut' became the triumphant highlight of her set, leaving "the crowd eating out of her hand and begging unsuccessfully for more."

In 2006, Yusuf received the Songwriter of the Year award from the American Society of Composers, Authors and Producers (ASCAP) for having written 'First Cut', which the award citation described as an "enduring classic". In 2014, Yusuf (as "Yusuf Islam a.k.a. Cat Stevens") was inducted into the Rock and Roll Hall of Fame in the Performers category, with 'First Cut' mentioned as a "modern standard" in his biography. Decades after their creation, the words of 'First Cut' are still speaking strongly and meaningfully.

The Worst that Could Happen
The 5th Dimension
1967

Hearing that your true love has married someone else is a devastating experience that you wouldn't wish on your worst enemy. (Unless you are a nasty, miserable excuse for a human being, in which case you should probably be reading a different book.) As music fans, we tend to want our favourite artists to be happy – but we also recognize that an artist's personal misery often results in great art. And so it is with Jimmy Webb's 'The Worst That Could Happen': a song that draws on Webb's own life events to brilliantly encapsulate the torment of someone else's happiness becoming your sadness.

Webb grew up in Oklahoma as the son of a Baptist preacher. Both of his parents were musicians, and the family regularly sang together at home and in church. "If you sing all the time," Webb has said, "particularly if you couple that with having an emotional, religious experience - somewhere in there is the alchemy of 'Why don't I make up a song of my own'." After his parents went to sleep at night, Webb would "lean out of bed, flip on the radio, and cruise through the night" enchanted by pop songs by the likes of Gerry Goffin & Carole King, Barry Mann & Cynthia Weill, Neil Sedaka, and Bobby Vinton.

Webb started writing his own songs around the age of 12; "songwriting was therapy and a personal refuge for a rather shy youngster, often picked on for being a PK [preacher's kid] and mercilessly teased about glasses and pimples." He moved to California with his family as a teenager, and stayed there after his mother's death, in the same year that he graduated from high school and the rest of his family moved back to Oklahoma. "I was a professional songwriter by 17, but not because I had designed to be. It was because that was the only commodity I had. I had no money but I did have songs."

At 18, Webb was hired as a staff writer for Jobete, Motown Records' publishing company. His first recorded track was 'My Christmas Tree' on the Supremes '65 album *Merry Christmas*; he characterized his strategy at Jobete as "setting up for artists who'd had hits and saying 'I'm gonna write the follow up to that'. You could, kinda, insert yourself - slide in there - between the first record and the next record. This is the way you insinuated yourself into the process." He left Jobete to sign with Johnny Rivers' music publishing company - but, as Webb describes in his autobiography *The Cake and the Rain*, he was somewhat at loose ends when Rivers asked him to work with the Versatiles, a group managed by Motown executive Marc Gordon. Webb was impressed by the group because "there was no sense of 'band uniform' like most of the Motown acts had. Here was this black group that had thrown all that away and were dressing very individually. And here was this beautiful sound of a blend of girls' and boys' voices. We had five people, so we could do very rich, close harmony, from a more traditional era."

The Versatiles became The 5th Dimension, and gained attention in late '66 with a cover of The Mamas & The Papas' 'Go Where You Wanna Go'. Then, while Rivers was away on tour, Webb worked with the group on an arrangement of his own song, the breezy 'Up, Up and Away'. "I was a little nervous about that 'cause [Rivers] could be very volatile." However, Rivers liked the song, and it not only became a US Top 10 hit in '67, but also became the title track of The 5th Dimension's first album on Rivers' Soul City Records. The group's second album was to have been produced by Rivers, but problems between Rivers and the group led to arranger Bones Howe asking Webb to work on the album Howe had named *The Magic Garden*. Howe envisioned the album as "the Jimmy Webb album": a "song cycle" weaving together Webb's arrangements and songs, including a new number, 'The Worst That Could Happen'. In retrospect, Webb said, "*The Magic Garden* was designed to be cohesive, and though the connections between the songs are not obvious, they were all inspired by the same romantic situation."

That situation was Webb's passionate but turbulent relationship with his high school girlfriend Suzy Horton. Webb describes her in *The Cake and the Rain* as "the closest thing I ever had to a childhood sweetheart…She was the quintessential California blonde, with a stunning figure, large blue eyes, and a sweet smile." Horton was also a part of the four-woman quartet The Contessas, put together by Webb in '65 while he and Horton were in junior college. The group released a single with two of his songs, 'This is Where I Came In' and 'I Keep on Keepin' On', but broke up shortly afterwards. Horton moved to Nevada to pursue a career as a professional dancer, and met the man who became her first husband. Finding out about their marriage was the event that inspired Webb to write 'The Worst That Could Happen'.

In his '98 book *Tunesmith: Inside the Art of Songwriting*, Webb describes 'The Worst That Could Happen' as being structured like a series of connected and increasingly elaborate rooms. "The verse begins a story or chain of reasoning that leads to an expository statement, much like an elegant foyer prepares the visitor for an entrance into a large and impressive room full of architectural detail and significance." He also depicts the song visually as a sequence of rising waves: to steal a poetic phrase, wave after wave, each mightier than the last. "Songwriters," he says, "are quite shamelessly playing with the emotions of human beings when we do this and it is a dirty job, but someone has to do it."

The sweeping crescendos and raw emotions of 'The Worst That Could Happen' were ideally suited to the commanding voice of The 5th Dimension's Billy Davis Jr., who sang lead on the track. Although 'Paper Cup' was chosen as the single from *The Magic Garden*, 'The Worst That Could Happen' was among the group's favourite tracks on the album. However, in '69 a version of the song by Johnny Maestro and The Brooklyn Bridge, which sounded almost identical to The 5th Dimension's version, reached #3 in the US charts. 'The Worst That Could Happen' might have seemed the ideal choice as another single from *The Magic Garden*, but the success of The Brooklyn Bridge's version likely pre-empted any possibility that The 5th Dimension's version could be a hit. However, that didn't stop Soul City from jumping on the bandwagon of The Brooklyn Bridge's success; Soul City re-released *The Magic Garden* under the title of, you guessed it, *The Worst That Could Happen*.

However, one listener – the subject of the song – was not thrilled by its success. 'The Worst That Could Happen' was one of "countless" songs that Webb wrote about Horton (the others include 'Wichita Lineman', 'By The Time I Get to Phoenix', and 'MacArthur Park'). Webb admits in *The Cake and the Rain* that Horton was bothered by his ongoing musical declarations of unrequited love, which were "a devastating and constant psychological weapon on the radio."

'The Worst That Could Happen' was covered several times, in '69 and later, by a variety of acts including the Lettermen, BJ Thomas, and J. Vincent Edwards. It also regularly showed up on records by groups like the Johnny Mann Singers, who specialized in softening popular songs into "easy listening". Even the more musically adventurous acts that covered the song, like Tinkerbells

Fairydust and The Goodees, kept their interpretations fairly close to Webb's original arrangement. 'The Worst That Could Happen' also became a hit in the Philippines in the mid-'70s, translated into Tagalog as 'Panakip-butas' (a metaphorical phrase describing someone who is a substitute or a second choice) and sung by Hajji Alejandro, billed as "today's hottest singing sensation!" when he performed 'Panakip-butas' in the '77 film of the same name.

The most different version, surprisingly, may be Webb's own rendition from '96's *Ten Easy Pieces*, an album on which he performed songs he had written that had been hits for other artists. Webb is definitely not a shouter when he sings, so his rendition of 'The Worst That Could Happen' is an intimate, low-key affair foregrounded by just his voice and piano. Not surprisingly, given his personal affinity with the song, the toned-down arrangement works remarkably well even without the usual melodramatic vocalizing.

Webb reveals in *The Cake and the Rain* that Horton's mother regularly telephoned him to let him know when Horton was encountering difficulties in that first marriage. When Horton and her husband eventually separated, Webb seized the opportunity to rekindle the flame. They became a couple again in the early '70s, when Webb was floundering professionally; his "pop songsmith" sensibilities didn't fit in with the folk and rock that was dominating the charts, and he felt he wasn't taken seriously when he tried writing topical songs. "I started doing songs about the environment and sex and all kinds of things that didn't exactly fit the middle of the road. It became obvious very quickly that the artists who had been fantastically successful with my early work were not going to do these songs." He recorded several albums of his own work, which received critical praise but didn't sell well.

Webb then fell in with a crowd of notorious Los Angeles showbiz partiers, including Harry Nilsson. At one point Nilsson "borrowed" Webb's brand-new Jaguar car, spent two weeks driving it across the US, flattened it, and then shipped it back to Webb on a truck. Webb's carousing, philandering, and drug use – he nearly overdosed on angel dust in '73 – were eventually too much for Horton, and she left him. She went on to develop a musical career of her own, married Linda Ronstadt's cousin Bobby, and now performs with him and former Stone Poneys member Bobby Kimmel in the group I Hear Voices!.

Webb got control over his life and settled down, continuing to write and also to perform as a solo artist. He has written works for musical theatre and for orchestras, as well as overseeing the legacy of his vast musical catalogue. In May 2018, his work was recognized in a "Celebration of Jimmy Webb" concert at Carnegie Hall. The event was staged as a fundraiser for research into Alzheimer's disease, the terrible condition that in August 2017 claimed Webb's "brother in music" Glen Campbell. One of the highlights of the show was Billy Davis Jr.'s soaring rendition of 'The Worst That Could Happen'.

While romantic anguish inspired 'The Worst That Could Happen', the story of the relationship behind the song actually has – well, not a traditional happy fairytale ending, but a resolution in a connection of mutual respect and affection. "Jimmy's songs have followed me my whole life," Horton told the *Los Angeles Times* in 2013, "and we are still friends to this day. Jimmy has a lovely wife and I have a wonderful husband. They have both had to deal with our histories. I mean no disrespect to anyone but I have to say, I have loved Jimmy for 50 years and I always will."

**Living Without You
Randy Newman
1968**

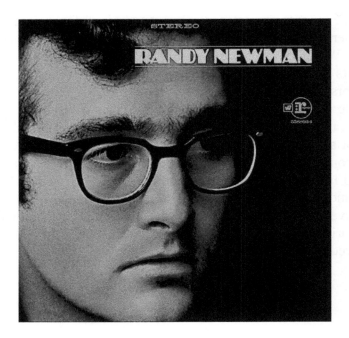

"He can communicate complex human emotions with just a few perfectly chosen words." That's how record producer and music industry executive Lenny Waronker, Randy Newman's friend since childhood, explains the brilliance of Newman's songwriting. Throughout his lengthy career, Newman's evocative ability has perhaps been best demonstrated by his songs about romantic heartbreak – and one fine example is 'Living Without You', from his '68 debut album.

Newman came from a family with a storied musical heritage. Three of his uncles (Alfred, Emil, and Lionel) were renowed composers, arrangers and conductors in the Hollywood film industry, and as a youngster Newman would be taken to soundstages to watch his uncles conduct large orchestras. Newman's mother was from New Orleans, and Newman spent his summers there, listening to the varied sounds of that musical city. Described by his brother Alan as "a lonely guy, no girlfriends", Newman started writing his own songs in his mid-teens, alone at a piano in his bedroom at home. With Waronker's encouragement, Newman started pitching his songs to artists at Liberty Records, which was owned by Waronker's father.

After Newman's song 'Somebody's Waiting' became the B-side to Gene McDaniels' single 'Spanish Lace', he was hired as an in-house songwriter by the publishing company Metric Music. While at Metric, Newman had songs covered by artists such as Gene Pitney ('Just One Smile', 'Nobody Needs Your Love'), Cilla Black ('I've Been Wrong Before', which he called "the best of the bunch" from that time) and the Walker Brothers ('I Don't Want to Hear It Any More'). He also co-wrote several songs with fellow Metric writer Jackie DeShannon, and followed in his uncles' footsteps by composing music for TV shows and films, including a collaboration with Bobby Darin on 'Look At Me' for the '64 car-centric film *The Lively Set*. One of Newman's other compositions, 'Looking at Me', was first recorded by Vic Dana and then covered by a Japanese group whose name he never found out – not even after he received a "big cheque" when the record was an overseas hit.

Newman released a single of his own in '62 – 'Golden Gridiron Boy', co-produced by Pat Boone – but since he felt, in his brother's words, that he himself sang "like shit", he was generally content to write songs for others. Newman did admit, though, in retrospect that "you expect that they'll do your songs better than you could." In '66, Waronker became an executive at Reprise Records, a subsidiary of Warner Bros. Records, and persuaded Newman to sign to Reprise as a recording artist.

It may have seemed counter-intuitive to sign an artist in his early 20s who had made one unsuccessful single and had almost no experience performing live, but, as Warners VP Joe Smith explained, "we would sooner go down in flames with an artist like Randy Newman than take a shot on a singles group that has a couple of hits and no long-term staying power." Waronker had also noticed that Newman's songwriting was starting to move in a different direction: "At first he was much more tune conscious. And then out of the blue he wrote a batch of songs that were completely different, titles like 'Mama Told Me Not to Come,' 'Bet No One Ever Hurt This Bad,' and 'I Think It's Going to Rain Today'. It was great, like a beautiful fusion of words and music."

Waronker enlisted Van Dyke Parks, another Reprise artist, to co-produce Newman's first album. Parks, in addition to being a performer, was also a songwriter, composer, and arranger, and had covered Newman's 'Vine Street' on his own debut album,'67's *Song Cycle*. Waronker has stated that Newman, influenced by the Beach Boys' *Pet Sounds* and the Beatles' *Sgt. Pepper*, was "intrigued" by the idea of building an album around orchestration. "The concept was to present Randy's take on orchestra, with a minimal amount of backbeat, at a time when rock'n'roll was still evolving...it was incredibly ambitious." It was also decidedly against the musical trends of the time. Parks says, "It was consciously counter-counter-culture. We knew that. It was squaresville to use an orchestra." Newman wrote all of the arrangements on the album, and, with his uncle Alfred, conducted the orchestra during the recording sessions.

'Living Without You' is less embellished than some of the album's other tracks, but that minimalism perfectly suits its despondency. In the space of three minutes, Newman completely inhabits the character of the abandoned, awkward outsider bemoaning his loneliness; the mood of pathos is intensified by sparse, repetitive piano chords amidst almost mockingly cheerful instrumentation.

On its initial release in '68, *Randy Newman* (also known as *Randy Newman Creates Something New Under the Sun*) received positive reviews, but sold less than 5,000 copies. Newman was also dismayed with the initial packaging of the album; as Parks recounted, "The clever liner notes man referred to Randy as a 'pudgy Hoagy Carmichael'. Nothing could have broken Randy's heart more. As his father pointed out, Hoagy Carmichael was an anti-Semite. So we quickly changed that cover and came out with another."

A re-release of the album the following year did not significantly increase the album's sales, even with an advertising campaign that wryly promised "Once You Get Used To It, His Voice Is Really Something". Reflecting on the album in '74, Newman mused, "It was difficult for people to follow, y'know…but I felt I also learnt more about how to accompany my voice during the course of making the record."

More recent observers have noted that the quirkiness of the first album also outlined the directions of much of Newman's subsequent work: "Poignant songs about romantic longing were juxtaposed with character-driven vignettes, darkly irreverent commentaries on the human condition and quirky tunes of ambiguous meaning. In time all those modes would be refined, all those subjects explored." Parks is more straightforward about the greater impact of the album. "There is nothing like this record for its individuality and beauty. A sense of piquancy in the blues, laced with sorrow. A sense of humour in the face of sorrow, a defiant humour. This record is a milestone in its influence on other artists of that time."

On its own, 'Living Without You' has been somewhat overshadowed by Newman's more successful songs from that album, such as 'Davy the Fat Boy' and 'I Think It's Going To Rain Today'. But as documented on *Live at the Boarding House '72* - recorded during a promotional tour for *Sail Away*, Newman's third album - 'Living Without You' was part of Newman's concerts for several years after its release.

The first two artists to cover 'Living Without You' actually did so before the release of Newman's own version. The first was Keith Shields, the lead singer of the Wildcats, a popular live act in Northumberland. The Wildcats lineup also included guitarist Hilton Valentine, who went on to play with the Animals. In '67, after the Animals broke up, Valentine became Shields' manager and produced three singles for him. While none of those singles charted, the cover of Donovan's 'Hey Gyp (Dig the Slowness)' got some attention. But 'Living Without You' (credited as 'So Hard Living Without You') is also noteworthy, if only for being so radically different from Newman's rendition. The Shields/Valentine interpretation sounds much more a product of its era, with swirling wah-wah guitar and powerful vocals.

In early '67, Alan Price had a UK hit with his cover of Newman's 'Simon Smith and the Amazing Dancing Bear', and he obviously was a fan of Newman's work. Of the 13 tracks on Price's second album, *A Price on His Head* - released that same year – seven were by Newman, including three from the not-yet-released debut album: 'Living Without You', 'So Long Dad', and 'Bet No One Ever Hurt This Bad'. There's no orchestras here on 'Living Without You', just Price and his piano. Unlike Newman, Price keeps a steady beat throughout the track, and his jaunty vaudeville-tinged piano – aurally reminiscent of his arrangement for 'Simon Smith' – complements a rueful vocal. While Newman's version evokes a disheartened loner slowly waking up to face yet another dreary day, Price's interpretation is that of someone already awake, sadly musing over what went wrong.

Harry Nilsson included 'Living Without You' among the Newman songs he selected for his '70 album *Nilsson Sings Newman*. Newman collaborated on the making of the album, and perhaps not surprisingly, Nilsson's version hews close to Newman's original arrangement. Nilsson's slightly echoing double-tracked voice, nestled in his signature choral vocal settings, manages to be both lush and stark at the same time. The Nitty Gritty Dirt Band also covered the song in '70; this countrified rendition seems constrained by its rigid tempo, and somehow doesn't resonate quite as emotionally as other versions do.

Some Internet sources list another single of 'Living Without You' from '70, allegedly by Canadian musician Bill Henderson of The Collectors and Chilliwack. Further investigation indicates, however, that this is a different song by the same name, performed by a different Bill Henderson (the jazz vocalist) and with a different sardonic take on romantic breakups - namely, listing all the things that one can do again now that the ex is gone.

But back to Randy Newman's song. Manfred Mann (the band) had numerous well-documented evolutions since '62, through several formats, names, and lineups, before Manfred Mann (the bandleader) launched his Earth Band in '72. The Earth Band's first single was its "upbeat pop treatment" of 'Living Without You', which one reviewer tactfully evaluated as "quite nice". Any pain that the listener might experience while hearing this interpretation will not be from empathizing with the song's sad protagonist, but from cringing at the squonky synthesizer and bland vocals. Nevertheless, the Earth Band's 'Living Without You' managed to crack the Top 70 in the US, and thus helped to pave the way for the group's more adventurous and successful remakes later in the decade.

Newman himself revisited 'Living Without You' in 2003, for the first in his *Songbook* series of albums. 'Living Without You' is still occasionally part of Newman's live sets, but it's always intriguing to hear what a mature artist does in the studio with a song from when he was relatively young, and to hear whether time and experience have affected how he understands the song. The 2003 'Living Without You' arrangement is only piano and vocals, which shows off the wonderful unexpected turns in the song's instrumental structure – something that was largely obscured by the orchestration in the original version. Newman's voice is more weary, more contemplative, but he gently and achingly draws out what Ian MacDonald identified as the underlying theme of 'Living Without You': "the longing for the alleviation of simple, steady, dependable love". And that is something that listeners of any age can appreciate.

I'm the Urban Spaceman
Bonzo Dog Doo-Dah Band
1968

At the start of 1968, the Bonzo Dog Doo-Dah Band were described by their manager/producer Gerry Bron as "a cult band with a huge following, deservedly." Their live shows were chaotic sets of sardonic original tunes mixed with obscure comical songs from the '20s and '30s, all performed amidst "horror masks, weird instruments, explosions, and a life-size rag doll named Alma." Led by the eccentric charisma of frontman Viv Stanshall, the Bonzos were a popular live act everywhere from the club circuit in northern

England to premiere London venues such as UFO Club and the Marquee. The band had also acquired fans of all ages through regular television appearances on the ITV children's series *Do Not Adjust Your Set.*

But the Dadaist anarchy that made the Bonzos such entertaining performers did not translate into chart-friendly records. Their first three singles were failures, and Liberty, their UK record company, only pressed 2000 copies of their first LP *Gorilla.* According to singer/guitarist Neil Innes, "The record company was saying, 'Well, what about a single? What about a single?' And we couldn't care less. We were just still being silly art students."

As it happened, when the band went into the studio in autumn '68, Innes brought along a catchy ditty he had titled 'I'm the Urban Spaceman'. Innes' inspiration for the song came from two sources. One was the "urban spaces" of post-war rebuilding in Manchester: "They call them 'brownfield sites' nowadays. I just thought 'well, if there's urban space, why isn't there an urban spaceman?'" The other was the vacuous consumerism of '60s advertising: "shiny, smiley-faced people eating happy meals and things like this. And so the 'Urban Spaceman' was a composite of the sort of an ideal figure in an advert. He doesn't exist in real life." With a lilting melody inspired by the wailing "nananana" siren of a passing ambulance, 'I'm the Urban Spaceman' was very different from the Bonzos' usual wild pastiche of musical styles and ideas.

If the Bonzos had to have a single, 'I'm the Urban Spaceman' seemed a likely candidate. But the Bonzos' attempts to record the song were hampered by Bron, whose idea of effective record producing was to keep a strict schedule. If the band tried to work on anything for more than three hours, Bron's verdict was, "Right, that's it, we've got to move on to the next track." Then, one evening, Stanshall was out on the town with his friend Paul McCartney; the Beatles were fans of the Bonzos, and, the Bonzos had performed 'Death Cab For Cutie' in the Beatles' '67 television film *Magical Mystery Tour.* However, rather than having a delightful night out, Stanshall spent most of the evening complaining bitterly to McCartney about Bron's draconian production methods. McCartney responded by offering to produce 'I'm the Urban Spaceman'. The Bonzos accepted McCartney's offer because, in Innes' words, "that was the only way we were going to get Gerry off the control desk, to have somebody like Paul, who wasn't known as a record producer, but he was known."

When McCartney arrived at Chappell Studios in central London, where the Bonzos were recording, he immediately sat down at the piano and played 'Hey Jude', which he had just finished writing. This delighted the band, not only because they were likely the first audience ever to hear the song, but because they knew that such antics would greatly annoy the clock-watching Bron. McCartney then got the band to play through 'I'm the Urban Spaceman' several times, and went around and showed each musician a different way of playing their part that Innes says "made the whole thing take off". The Bonzos played their own instruments on the record, but McCartney allowed them to keep his ukulele track on the final version of the song. While McCartney was practicing his strumming, Bron's wife Lillian wandered by and asked, "What's that you've got there, a poor man's violin?" McCartney retorted, "No, it's a rich man's ukulele."

After an eight-hour recording session, both McCartney and the Bonzos were satisfied with how the song sounded. But the track still had to be mixed, and at that point the band's recording budget was nearly exhausted. However, engineer Gus Dudgeon had an idea. He had previously worked at Decca Studios in west London, and had left that job only a few months ago. So he tucked the 'Urban Spaceman' master tape under one arm, and casually strolled into Decca "where the doorman greeted him as if he had been off on holiday for a couple of weeks". Dudgeon then crept into the control room of a studio being used by the Moody Blues – who at that particular moment were taking a lunch break – and surreptitiously mixed 'I'm The Urban Spaceman'. Drummer 'Legs' Larry Smith explained, "He was kind enough to note all the fader positions and reset them afterwards so the Moodies weren't put out, or any the wiser."

Innes told McCartney biographer Howard Sounes, "I'd like to go on record as saying that the record would have been nothing like [as successful] without Paul's touch." And with McCartney's consent, the Bonzos took one final jibe at Bron's push for commercial success. They demanded that the production of the single be credited not to the famous Beatle, but to one "Apollo C. Vermouth".

'I'm the Urban Spaceman' was released in the UK in October '68. It spent 14 weeks on the UK charts, peaking at #5, and was the only Top 40 single the Bonzos ever had in the UK. According to Innes, after the true identity of "Apollo C. Vermouth" was revealed, the single sold as much as 18,000 copies in a day.

Liberty Records, in what can only be described as a "throw it at the wall and see if it sticks" marketing strategy, released 'I'm the Urban Spaceman' as a single in such unlikely markets as Greece, Spain, Rhodesia, South Africa, and New Zealand. Matters were further confused when, despite being a hit, 'I'm the Urban Spaceman' was not included on *The Doughnut in Granny's Greenhouse*, the album that resulted from the Bonzos' Chappell Studios sessions. In most of the world, including the UK, 'Spaceman' did not appear on a Bonzos album until *Tadpoles* was released the following year. Imperial Records, the Bonzos' American record label, initially wanted Stanshall's epic 'Canyons of Your Mind' as a single, but eventually were persuaded to go along with the rest of the world in releasing 'Spaceman' instead. 'Spaceman' was also added to the North American version of *The Doughnut in Granny's Greenhouse,* which was, smartly, retitled as *Urban Spaceman.*

Perversely, the band members decided that having a hit single in the UK meant they should go on tour in the US. The fed-up Bron promptly dumped them as management clients, and Stanshall enlisted the services of manager Tony Stratton-Smith. Stanshall was impressed by Stratton-Smith's success with The Nice, who, with their distinctive blend of rock and classical music, also did not fit traditional expectations of what a successful band should sound like.

Under Stratton-Smith's guidance, the Bonzos visited the US twice, but both tours were disastrous. Saxophone player Rodney Slater remembers that the band got minimal, if any, tour support from its management and record label. Stanshall complained that the band regularly encountered situations such as little or no publicity for shows, concert dates being changed without their knowledge, and large numbers of LPs being sent to record stores in cities where the band wasn't even booked to play. Then, during the second US tour, band member Roger Ruskin Spear's wife became seriously ill at home in the UK; for four days, Spears was unaware of frantic messages from his family, even though the messages were sent to the hotels the band were supposed to be staying at and also to the band's booking agency. When the band members finally found out what had been happening, that was the last straw. They were so angry that they cancelled the rest of the tour and flew back to the UK. Unfortunately, the cancelled dates included shows in several large US cities – shows that might have considerably raised the band's profile in North America. The Bonzos and Stratton-Smith went their separate ways not long after that, but author Johnny Rogan says that "the Bonzos proved a happy diversion from Stratton-Smith's more serious ventures, and his one regret was that, like the Nice, they failed to win strong support from their American record company."

Stanshall had a complicated relationship with 'I'm the Urban Spaceman', despite the attention it brought to the band. He was offended that the lyric "I've got speed" was interpreted as a reference to drugs, and he hated the "machinery of pop" that went along with having a hit single. In later years, he expressed disdain for the song, saying that being expected to play it "used to make me puke", and dismissing it as "an unacceptable gloss. There are and were other things that I'm more proud of." (Innes, though, has pointed out that Stanshall willingly composed the melody for, and played, the tenor recorder featured on the song.)

Despite the lilting charm of 'I'm the Urban Spaceman', it has rarely been recorded by other acts. But Innes has reworked the song for several subsequent projects. He performed 'Spaceman' in '75 on *Rutland Weekend Television*, his collaboration with Eric Idle on Idle's first post-Monty Python venture. Innes' appearance was presented as "a party political broadcast on behalf of the Conservative Party". In top hat and tails, clanging a foot-operated cymbal and playing a tinny portable keyboard, he sang the song while Lyn Ashley (Mrs. Idle at the time) tap-danced around him. Innes also re-recorded 'I'm The Urban Spaceman' with a Dixieland/trad jazz arrangement to accompany a sketch on his '79 TV series *Innes Book of Records*. In '82, as 'Carl Weetabix', Innes performed the song as part of an alleged "talent-spotting contest" in the Monty Python concert film *Live At The Hollywood Bowl,* with Python regular Carol Cleveland providing the tap-dancing accompaniment. Innes also often performs the song in his concert appearances.

Other acts have played 'I'm The Urban Spaceman' in concerts, and they are a mixed bag, to say the least. Mungo Jerry, of 'In The Summertime' fame, played 'Spaceman' as part of their set at the Weeley Festival in Clacton-on-Sea in '71; a review in the *New Musical Express* noted that "an Alsatian dog came and laid along the front of the stage, panting and shooting the odd glance at the band. He seemed to enjoy 'Urban Spaceman' and all the others as much as everyone else."

Ira Kaplan, the leader of the indie trio Yo La Tengo, is a self-admitted "fairly rabid" fan of Innes and the Bonzos. Yo La Tengo have backed Innes on some of his US tours, including contributing a backup chorus of kazoos to 'Spaceman', and Innes has occasionally joined the band when they have performed the song at their own shows. Graham Parker, whose stock in trade is fiery, piercingly brilliant songs, might not seem to be the type of artist who would appreciate the Bonzos' work, but he has been an admirer since the era of the "subversive" *Do Not Adjust Your Set*; he performs 'I'm the Urban Spaceman' in his shows as a "silly song" that's "the perfect antidote to all of my anger".

The songs of Richard Thompson, who's characterized the mood of his own writing as "doom and gloom from the tomb", also may seem very unlike the work of the Bonzos. But Thompson played guitar on Stanshall's '81 solo album *Teddy Boys Don't Knit*, and he also must have picked up some knowledge of the Bonzos' repertoire along the way, because he played 'I'm The Urban Spaceman' at one of his "all requests" solo shows in 2016. Appropriately, given the Bonzos' affinity for music from the '20s and '30s, the song has also found its way into the repertoires of several ukulele orchestras.

'I'm the Urban Spaceman' could be dismissed as a one-hit wonder and as not truly representative of the Bonzos' musical range and creativity. But the raucous audience singalong at the Bonzos' 50th anniversary concert in April 2015 showed that the song is still deeply loved. And for such a uniquely influential band as the

Bonzos, perhaps being remembered for one unrepresentative song is preferable to not being remembered at all.

Feelin' Alright?
Traffic/Joe Cocker
1968

'Feelin' Alright?' is a song about turmoil and uncertainty, and that's exactly what the song caused for both Dave Mason, its writer, and Joe Cocker, one of the first artists to cover it. For each of them, the song became a highlight of their careers, but they also expressed ambivalence about being so closely associated with it. Unquestionably, though, 'Feelin' Alright?' is a masterpiece, emerging from the hippie haze of the late '60s with an irresistibly funky rhythm that's inspired versions by more than 50 other acts.

Mason wrote the "two-chord classic" sometime in early '68, on a trip to the Greek island of Hydra in between his first and second stints in Traffic; Pete Frame describes Mason's participation in that band as being "in and out like a dog at a fair". The band's first album was a result of "getting back to the country", a creative process employed by several high-profile acts of the time, such as Led Zeppelin, The Band, and Fleetwood Mac. The band and its entourage would take up collective residence in a rural location, away from urban and commercial distractions, so as to focus solely on music-making. For their rural retreat, Traffic selected an isolated and reputedly haunted gatekeeper's cottage near Aston Tirrold in Berkshire (now in Oxfordshire). The woodshedding resulted in the landmark *Mr. Fantasy* album - but Mason quit the band before the album's release, feeling uncomfortable with "too much success too quick", and went his own way.

Then, when Traffic was on tour in the United States, they crossed paths with Mason at a New York airport. That chance encounter eventually brought Mason back into the fold, in time for the band's return to its country cottage to work on material for its next album. But rather than working collaboratively with the rest of Traffic's members, Mason brought in finished songs that he had completed on his own – and those songs were distinctly different from those that were being collectively created. Steve Winwood told *Rolling Stone* in '69 that Mason was not solely responsible for how 'Feelin' Alright?' turned out – "it was Dave's song, but he didn't create the mood" – while Mason later claimed that Winwood was jealous of Mason's ability to write "commercial" hits.

Not surprisingly, this tension eventually resulted in Mason again departing Traffic, right after its self-titled second album was released in October '68. 'Feelin' Alright?' was immediately recognized as one of the stronger tracks on the album, starting with Mason's pensive vocals and guitar, and then, with the addition of congas, saxophone, and piano, building into an exuberant jam. Although Mason said he thought 'You Can All Join In' would have been the best choice as a single from *Traffic*, 'Feelin' Alright?' was chosen instead, and was released as a single in several territories with 'Withering Tree' on the B-side. (A slightly different version of 'Withering Tree' later appeared on Traffic's '69 album *Last Exit*.)

Mason went on to release the highly-regarded *Alone Together* album and built a solid solo career, including a brief stint as a member of Fleetwood Mac. He also covered 'Feelin' Alright?'

himself on his '72 album *Headkeeper*. But even as early as '74 he was concerned about comparisons of his new work to his past successes: "It would mean making the same album again and again, and I don't want to have to cater. It's the same with 'Feelin' Alright?'. Everybody is waiting for another one. I got trapped into looking at my songs that way once and it got me crazy. Now, I can't conform to an image." He also complained that bad management deals had deprived him of much of what he could have earned from his earlier work. "The royalty [Traffic] were on was shit. In America it was worse – it was half of the English one. I don't even get my full writer's money for 'Feelin' Alright?', I finished up with half."

Three Dog Night and Joe Cocker both covered 'Feelin' Alright?' within a few months of *Traffic*'s release. Three Dog Night's version appeared on their second album, *Suitable for Framing,* in mid-'69. Although the track featured the horn section from Chicago and an outstandingly groovy organ, the reaction to their interpretation was generally lukewarm. The eventual hits 'Eli's Coming', 'Celebrate', and 'Easy to be Hard' received much more attention. ('Feelin' Alright?' later showed up as the B-side of the 'Celebrate' single.)

Within a few weeks, however, Cocker took the song to new heights on his debut album, *With A Little Help From My Friends*. Rather than opening the song gently, as Traffic and Three Dog Night did, his version blasted right off with the dramatic interplay of Artie Butler's rhythmic piano chords and Laudir's congas, punctuated by the distinctive "burrrrrr" of a vibraslap (best percussion instrument name ever). Cocker's brilliance as an interpreter was shown in that even as a soulful shouter he still conveyed the nervous edge that underlies the song's lyrics. "In Cocker's hands", wrote reviewer Bud Scoppa, "'Feeling Alright' was utterly transformed into a vision of raging paranoia." (Despite the uncertainty that Cocker so convincingly portrayed, the title of his version changed the song's original title by dropping the question mark at the end and making 'Feelin' into 'Feeling'.)

Although the title track of *With A Little Help From My Friends* became its big hit single, 'Feeling Alright' quickly became a staple of Cocker's live set. He performed it at Woodstock – where he introduced it as "sort of an English variation on somebody's head-bashin' tune" – and also on several US and UK television shows, which introduced viewers to his unique herky-jerky bodily contortions. The *New York Times* sniffed, "Rocking from side to side and jerking his arms around as if he were suffering some sort of seizure, Mr. Cocker is probably the only rock singer who belts out powerful, polished songs while imitating Boris Karloff." But even the NYT's snobby critic had to admit, "Mr. Cocker is happily both powerful and sensitive. With what he can do, he can be allowed a certain amount of unusual gesturing."

'Feeling Alright' was also prominently featured on the massive Mad Dogs and Englishmen tour in '70. The tour starred Cocker, musical director Leon Russell on piano, most of Delaney & Bonnie's backing band, and an ever-changing roster of hangers-on and liggers. Cocker had just over a week to pull together the tour, which was chronicled in both a concert film and a live album, and it turned out to be a harrowing and exhausting experience which ultimately lost money despite the high-profile performers that were involved. The quality of shows varied widely from night to night, because of the haphazard organization of the whole affair; the "choir" of vocalists supporting Cocker regularly included random individuals with backstage passes who decided to get up on stage and howl along with the pros. Nevertheless, the version of 'Feelin' Alright' that ended up on the live album demonstrates why the song was usually a highlight of Cocker's shows.

At the end of '72, Cocker told an interviewer, "It's daft the way audiences like hearing old numbers. I'd much rather hear anybody do new songs and it's pretty boring for me – there are some I'd like to wind down like 'Feeling Alright' and 'Hitchcock Railway'." But Cocker apparently still had enough of a sense of humour about his association with 'Feeling Alright' to perform it in '76 on the US TV show *Saturday Night Live*, alongside comedian John Belushi doing an uncannily accurate imitation of him.

Subsequent covers of 'Feeling Alright' seem to be either on Team Traffic or Team Cocker, depending on which arrangement they decide to follow. Some of the major exceptions include Grand Funk Railroad, on their '71 album *Survival*, who rendered parts of the song almost as a slow blues, with a stripped-down bass-heavy sound. On the cover of the album, the band also took "getting back to the country" to the extreme by smearing themselves with mud, donning loincloths, and crouching around a firepit in a rocky wilderness. Isaac Hayes' version of 'Feeling Alright' from '73 layers on wah-wah guitar, horns, and cooing backup singers, but it's epic. (If you feel like spending a few minutes in a weird alternate reality, go to YouTube and watch Hayes performing the song on TV with….the Osmonds.) Huey Lewis' version from the soundtrack of the 2000 film *Duets* definitely aligns with Team Cocker, but has surprising depth and swagger. In 2012, Cocker and Lewis toured together, and regularly duetted on 'Feeling Alright'.

In addition to recording the song himself, Mason himself has recorded 'Feeling Alright' with fellow Traffic alumnus Jim Capaldi and as a guest with other acts such as the Tedeschi Trucks Band. Interestingly, when Mason, Capaldi, and Winwood put their differences aside long enough for Traffic to be inducted into the Rock and Roll Hall of Fame in 2004, their performance of 'Feeling Alright' hewed closer to Cocker's arrangement than to their own original. But it's their song, so hey, why not? As the song itself says, "that was then and now I'm here today."

Think of Rain
Margo Guryan
1968

'Think of Rain' is one of those songs that, upon hearing it, you wonder, "Why on earth wasn't this a massive hit?" It's charming, it's catchy, it's exquisitely produced and arranged, and Guryan's dreamy vocals perfectly match its mood of whimsical romance. But even though it was covered several times in the mid-'60s, 'Think of Rain' remained largely overlooked for many years. Thankfully, subsequent re-releases of Guryan's work have resulted in this sunshine-pop gem getting the appreciation it deserves.

Guryan grew up in a musical household in Far Rockaway, a small town not far from New York City. Her parents were both pianists; her mother had studied piano at university, and her father was an enthusiastic amateur musician. Their home also had a Victrola and a radio that brought all kinds of music into the house. Guryan herself started piano lessons at age six. Encouraged by her parents, she wrote songs as a child; she regularly wrote poems for family occasions, and then, as she learned piano, she found it natural to put melodies to her words. She loved the compositions of Bach and Scarlatti, and in her teens she developed an interest in jazz after her father bought her George Shearing's album *East of the Sun*. She studied piano and composition at Boston University, and also had lessons with jazz pianist and instrumentalist Jaki Byard.

During '57, her first year at university, Guryan signed to Atlantic Records as a singer/songwriter. A club owner in Boston had offered her a recording contract, but on the advice of a lawyer, she and her parents sought out bigger opportunities in New York City. After Atlantic owners Jerry Wexler and Ahmet Ertegun heard her play some of her original songs, they signed her to their label. In a brief item announcing the signing, *Billboard* magazine described her as a "thrush, pianist, [and] cleffer" [industry slang for 'songwriter'] and mentioned the imminent release of an album, *Margo Guryan Singing Her Own Songs*. However, she says, "The only session I did for them was a total disaster," and the album never happened. But in '58 her composition 'Moon Ride' was recorded by a fellow Atlantic artist, jazz singer Chris Connor, and that gave her the impetus to keep writing songs.

Guryan was chosen to attend the Lenox School of Jazz in '59 and '60, in a summer program that brought together established musicians and promising students. At Lenox, she had the opportunity to work with jazz legends Max Roach and Milt Jackson; her classmates included Ornette Coleman and Don Cherry. Connections made there resulted in her writing the liner notes for Roach's '61 album *Percussion Bitter Sweet*, and her song 'On My Way to Saturday' being recorded in '62 by Harry Belafonte.

Guryan's musical direction changed in '66 when she became fascinated by the Beach Boys' *Pet Sounds* album. "It was a theory lesson. I learned that the bass note wasn't necessarily part of a determined chord - it could actually *determine* the chord. By doing that, the direction of the song might change and offer options you'd never have thought of otherwise." And 'God Only Knows' in particular provided her with a spark of inspiration. "I played that song over and over again, and then sat down at the piano and wrote 'Think of Rain'".

But it turned out to be a challenge to record 'Think of Rain' the way Guryan wanted it to sound. The song was initially demoed with other singers doing the lead vocal. Guryan recalls that "they had lovely voices, but screwed up the 'time'. I often change time signatures within a song, and they would 'straighten out' my 3/4 measures to 4/4...utterly ruining the song." Guryan pleaded with her music publisher (and future husband), David Rosner, "to let me try to sing on it. In the studio he said, 'Let's try doubling her voice', and it turned out that I was good at it! I would sing on one track, put earphones on as they played it back, and match the first vocal almost exactly."

Rosner also told her that the song needed an "arrangement", so Guryan wrote one. "That was truly a learning experience. I wrote out *everything*. The musicians didn't seem to mind...except for the drummer. I forget who he was...but when it was straight 4/4 he was fine. When it came to a break, I don't think he very much liked what I had written. He...played...it...exactly. No feel at all. I never did THAT again!"

The demo of the song, with Guryan's double-tracked vocals, quickly attracted attention from other artists and from music publishers. In '67 'Think of Rain' was popular enough to be recorded four times: as an album track by Claudine Longet (*The Look of Love*) and by Jackie deShannon (*For You*), and as a single by Bobby Sherman and by Lesley Miller. Guryan notes that Miller's producer husband, Alan Lorber, actually purchased the demo track of 'Think of Rain', and so Miller's single is the demo's instrumental track with Miller's vocals on top.

Another Guryan composition, 'Sunday Mornin'', was recorded in late '67 by Spanky and Our Gang, and became a Top 30 hit in the US. That success, plus Rosner promoting Guryan's demos to his music industry contacts, led to a few record companies expressing interest in signing Guryan as an artist. Guryan and Rosner eventually chose to sign with Bell Records, which at the time was home to high-profile acts such as the Box Tops, the Delfonics, and Merrilee Rush. Guryan's first album for Bell, *Take A Picture,* was initially going to be produced by John Simon, who had previously recorded an unreleased version of 'Think of Rain' with The Cyrkle. However, soon after started, Simon left to work with Janis Joplin – "who could blame him?" says Guryan – though his arrangement of 'Don't Go Away' made it onto the final version of the album.

John Hill took over the recording project and produced the rest of *Take A Picture*, although the album version of 'Think of Rain' is the demo track enhanced with a new string arrangement by Guryan. "When it came to recording it for the album, nothing matched the grace of the demo. [For the arrangement] I was getting away from the 'jazz feel' sort of music I had been writing. I was simply trying to write an arrangement which would allow the song to blend into the marvelous array of music being produced at that time."

Take A Picture came out in '68, with the title track backed with 'What Can I Give You' as a single. Bell also released a second single by Guryan, a non-album track called 'Spanky & Our Gang' – a shout-out to that band – backed with 'Sunday Mornin''. The album and the singles received positive reactions – *Record World* described 'Spanky & Our Gang' as "girlishly enchanting". But none of these releases were hits, partly because Guryan was reluctant to go on tour. She told Bell Records president Larry Utall that she was not interested in doing promotional appearances; what she wanted to do was to write songs. In her words, "All promotion was then stopped, and the record tanked." Guryan also modestly attributes *Take A Picture*'s lack of commercial success to there being "so many [other] wonderful artists and groups in the late '60s."

Take A Picture turned out to be not only Guryan's first album for Bell, but also her last. She and the company parted ways not long after its release. However, 'Think of Rain' continued to have a life of its own. It was subsequently recorded in '69 by the Split Level and by Astrud Gilberto in '70, along with an unreleased version by Dion. It was also translated into Swedish and recorded in '70 by the duo of Lill Lindfors and Svante Thuresson, who had gained some previous fame by placing second in the '66 Eurovision song competition.

Harry Nilsson, whose work Guryan greatly admired, also covered 'Think of Rain', but his version was never released and Guryan sadly never got to hear it. "He promised he would let me hear it, but we learned that although the song was listed on a tape box it was spliced out by Harry. Apparently he did that when he was unhappy with something he had recorded." For a long time, Guryan's favourite cover of the song was Jackie deShannon's – "because the arrangement was so different from my demo arrangement" – but her more recent favourite interpretation is the one by New Zealand singer Malcolm McNeill, which can be heard on YouTube. "The arrangement is totally original, and quite different from mine. The piano accompaniment is quite beautiful and Malcolm's vocal is flawless."

Other tracks from *Take A Picture* were covered by Carmen McRae ('Don't Go Away' and 'Can't You Tell' on her '68 album *The Sound of Silence*) and Julie London ('Sunday Mornin'' and 'Come to Me Slowly' on '69's *Yummy Yummy Yummy*). Another version of 'Sunday Mornin'', by Oliver, was a US Top 40 hit in '69. Guryan subsequently placed songs with several other artists, including Claudine Longet ('I Don't Intend to Spend Christmas Without You', also later recorded by Saint Etienne), Cass Elliot ('I Think A Lot About You'), and the Lennon Sisters ('I Love'). Although Guryan continued to write songs into the '70s, she gradually moved away from recording and developed a career as a piano teacher in Los Angeles.

Take A Picture became something of a legendary rare album, partly because original copies of it were so hard to find. After Bell Records essentially disowned the album, it made its way into the bargain bins – Guryan herself saw copies of it on sale for 39 cents - and then disappeared from sight. By the late '80s, an original copy of *Take A Picture* would change hands for around $200 US on the collector market. Then in the early '90s Japanese fans discovered the album, and thousands of bootleg copies were sold in that country. Finally, in 2000, the album was belatedly recognized as the "soft-rock gem" that it is, and *Take A Picture* was officially re-released by independent labels in the US, Japan and Spain. The full set of Guryan's demos for *Take A Picture* were later released on 2001's *25 Demos* (which, with additional tracks, appeared as

Thoughts the following year), on 2014's *27 Demos*, and on 2016's *29 Demos*. *Take A Picture* was also re-released on vinyl in 2018.

While Guryan has collaborated on some musical projects since *Take A Picture* was first re-released, her only other solo album is 2009's *The Chopsticks Variations*, a set of instrumentals inspired by her piano students. "They all loved the Mozart variations on 'Twinkle, Twinkle Little Star' ('Ah, vous dirai-je, Maman'). But the Mozart variations became too difficult too quickly. I wondered what I could write that would amuse them - aha! 'Chopsticks'! I was overwhelmed when Gunther Schuller, a Pulitzer Prize -winning composer, gave me a favorable quote for the manuscript."

Guryan still lives in Los Angeles, and while she still plays piano for her own enjoyment, she has only recently finished her teaching career. "I down-sized quite a bit over the last few years. In the past, I've found it fun to figure what kind of music a child, teenager or adult found compelling, and focus on that. At the same time as they were learning reading and counting, chord structure and fake-books could be incorporated. But my last student, a very talented young lady, has now gone off to college…leaving me officially retired!"

**Abergavenny
Marty Wilde/Shannon
1969**

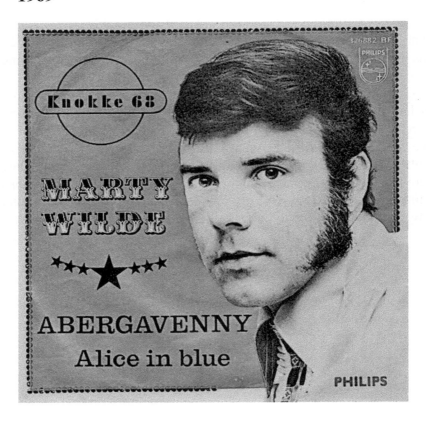

By the late '60s, Beatlemania and the Summer of Love had delivered a one-two punch to the careers of many artists who were stars earlier in the decade. As TV impresario Jack Good put it, "they were all-round entertainers with nobody left to entertain." Some resigned themselves to appearances on the supper club circuit and at nostalgia concerts. Others grew out their hair, donned paisley-print tunics and headbands, and jumped on the psychedelic bandwagon.

But more often than not, the music that resulted from the psychedelic reinventions was cringeworthy.

It would be easy to label Marty Wilde's '69 album *Diversions* as an example of that kind of desperate opportunism, but that label would be wrong – because, from the start of his career, Wilde had demonstrated a chameleonic ability to adapt. The former Reginald Smith had already refashioned himself as Reginald Patterson when in '57 he was recruited into manager Larry Parnes' stable of evocatively-surnamed teen idols. Parnes explained, "He was six-foot-four and looked quite tough and I thought, well, he's got to have a genteel first name so that it doesn't worry anybody. At the time there was a film out called *Marty* which was about this friendly character – so hence I said it was definitely to be Marty. Then, in order to get his sex appeal across – 'Wild' but with an 'E' on the end for superstition."

Wilde was promptly booked onto Parnes' famous package tours featuring multiple acts, with each performer given only a few songs in which to make an impression. He quickly became known as a dynamic live entertainer; even his rival Cliff Richard admitted, "I wasn't very good. Marty would have been far better to place the crown on." Wilde also regularly appeared on high-profile TV pop shows, including the BBC's *6.5 Special* and Good's *Oh Boy!* and *Boy Meets Girls*, and his television performances were admired for his charisma and his ability to convincingly handle varying musical styles. But producer Mickie Most astutely observed, "[h]e struggled because he was always doing other people's songs...and it wasn't until he wrote 'Bad Boy' [in '59] that he started to create his own thing."

However, in '59 Wilde married his wife Joyce, thus alienating the female teenage fans that expected their idols to be single and (theoretically) available. He acquired new fans by venturing into other areas of showbiz, including playing Conrad Birdie in the original West End production of the musical *Bye Bye Birdie*. But his string of UK Top 40 singles ended in '62, by which time he and Joyce had two small children. He later told a BBC interviewer, "[by then] it wasn't just me, it was a family to support. I used to really sweat – I've got to get this money for the mortgage, what am I going to do?" He continued to sporadically record and perform, including a stint in the mid-'60s with The Wilde Three: himself, Joyce (a former member of the Vernons Girls singing group), and a 16-year-old guitarist recruited through an ad in *Melody Maker* - future Moody Blues member Justin Hayward.

But Wilde also simultaneously developed a solid career as a songwriter. He wrote under his own name, sometimes under the pseudonym of "Frere Manston", and sometimes in partnership with Ronnie Scott (an agent and musical promoter, not the owner of the famed jazz club). In late '68, three songs that Wilde authored or co-authored were on the UK charts at the same time: Lulu's 'I'm a Tiger', Status Quo's 'Ice in the Sun', and the Casuals' 'Jesamine'. That success gave Wilde the opportunity to create *Diversions*, an album of him performing his own songs - and that in turn led to his unlikely hit single 'Abergavenny'.

Shockingly, *Diversions* has never been officially re-released – which is all the more shameful because of its musical versatility and consistently strong songwriting. (The audio of most of its tracks can be heard on YouTube, and an unofficial version with extra tracks came out on CD in 2018.) Admittedly, the cover of *Diversions*, with a photograph of Wilde in sideburns and mirrored round sunglasses, surrounded by swirling colorful figures and patterns, looks like your bog-standard "squares with beads on" effort. And while *Diversions* is not completely "psychedelic" – the softer songs such as 'Any Day' and 'Lullaby' are certainly no threat to the likes of Pink Floyd – the more adventurous numbers such as 'Zobo (1871-1892)' and 'Jesamine' can hold their own against many better-known tracks from the same era.

'Abergavenny' manages to be both contemporary and retro, in the style that Rob Chapman calls "psychedelic music hall". Its jaunty marching-band melody, with brassy orchestration by Peter Knight (who had just finished conducting the orchestra on the Moody Blues' *Days of Future Passed*), bounces alongside cheerful lyrics about a happy day out, with knowing winks to "trips" and "paradise people". Chapman, in his book *Psychedelia and Other Colours*, characterizes 'Abergavenny' thus: "Set to a pounding beat with trilling piccolo and oompah brass, [it is] a bracing and carefree homage to unfashionable seaside resorts, with just enough archly enunciated innuendo to give it some analogous cachet."

Perhaps by '69 some audiences had had enough of faux-Edwardian pop ditties, as 'Abergavenny' failed to make the UK charts. It became a Top 10 hit in Australia and also charted in several European countries – but where 'Abergavenny' found its biggest success was in North America, following in the footsteps of earlier Anglophiliac novelty tunes such as the New Vaudeville Band's 'Winchester Cathedral' and Herman's Hermits' 'I'm Henry VII, I Am'.

Puzzlingly, though, Wilde's US label, Heritage Records, released 'Abergavenny' under the pseudonym of Shannon – an odd decision, since 'Bad Boy' had been Wilde's only North American hit and a minor one at that. There was not much risk that American record-buyers would be confused by Wilde's change in musical personae. In addition, Heritage burdened the single with a cheap-looking sleeve, featuring a painfully "hip" typeface alongside an image of a mournful-looking tattered toy dog. What this poor doggy had to do with Abergavenny the song, Abergavenny the place, Wilde himself, or the pseudonymous Shannon is anyone's guess. Nevertheless, 'Abergavenny' reached the Top 50 in the US and Canada, and was a Top 25 Adult Contemporary hit in the US.

That success, plus the undeniable charm of the song's lilting melody, led to 'Abergavenny' being adapted into a wide range of foreign-language cover versions – many of which didn't directly translate the original English words, but instead built on the melody's evocation of fun and festivity. Claude François, who wrote the French-language song that in English became 'My Way', reworked 'Abergavenny' as 'Les Majorettes'. The YouTube video of his TV performance of the song, with dancing girls and baton twirlers, is definitely worth viewing. Another version in French, 'Le Cirque', came from Québecois pop star Normand Gélinas. There were versions in Italian (Samuela's 'Aria di Festa' and Antoine's 'Abracadabra') German (Ilja Richter's 'Ich Hol' Dir Gerne Vom Himmel Die Sterne'), Spanish (Karina's 'La Fiesta'), and Swedish (Ewa Roos' 'Kebnekajse'). There was an exotica version by Arthur Lyman, a rocking Hammond organ rendition by Harry Stoneham, and even an accordion version by the Dutch trio The 3 Jacksons.

But possibly the quirkiest cover version came from Brazil in the mid-'80s, where 'Abergavenny' was reworked into 'Pa-Ra-Tchi-

Bum', a cheerful song about watching a parade, for the children's TV show *Balão Mágico*. The five young stars of the show included Michael Biggs, the son of fugitive bank robber Ronnie and his Brazilian girlfriend. When Ronnie Biggs was kidnapped in '81, Michael went on Brazilian TV to plead for his father's safe return; the head of CBS Records in Brazil saw him on the news and thought he would be a good fit for the then-developing show. When *Balão Mágico* was launched, it became massively popular, and the five cast members then became a musical group, Turma do Balão Mágico (the "Magic Balloon Gang"). Michael Biggs described them as "Brazil's first boy band". The group's albums collectively sold more than 13 million copies, and 'Pa-Ra-Tchi-Bum' was featured on their final release in '86.

There was a second single from *Diversions*, 'The World Stood Up', and 'Any Day' from the album became the B-side to Wilde's '69 single 'Shelley'. 'It's So Unreal' also showed up on the B-side of the '71 single 'The Busker'. But after that, apart from the occasional compilation album, Wilde's own recording career was largely dormant as he focused on writing and producing records for his son Ricky, who was being pushed as the UK's equivalent to pre-teen dreamboy Jimmy Osmond. Then in '73 Wilde signed to Magnet Records, co-founded by his songwriting collaborator Peter Shelley.

He turned down the opportunity to record 'My Coo-Ca-Choo', and the song was passed along to his former Parnes stablemate Shane Fenton – who, as Alvin Stardust, had a huge hit with it. Wilde instead re-invented himself as glam rocker Zappo, and released the single 'Rock'n'Roll Crazy', telling *Record Mirror* that he wanted people to buy the record because they liked it "rather than because of having a following". Glam rock historian Dave Thompson observes rather snarkily that "the following had not bought one of his records since '62 and would pass this one by as well". 'Rock'n'Roll Crazy' was dire even by glam-rock standards, and it sank without a trace.

Wilde and Shelley went on to write and produce releases for other Magnet acts, such as the lone 45s by Ruby Pearl and the Dreamboats and by the Dazzling All Night Rock Show (both of which, according to Internet scuttlebutt, may also feature Wilde as a vocalist). Wilde himself released two '74 singles on Magnet - 'All Night Girl' and 'I Love You' – and Shannon made one last appearance in '75 with the unsuccessful 'Come Back and Love Me'. Wilde rediscovered his commercial mojo in '81 when he co-wrote 'Kids in America' for his daughter Kim; he has subsequently continued working with her and his other children, he regularly performs live, and he received an MBE in 2015 for "services to Popular Music".

While 'Abergavenny' and *Diversions* may be something of, well, a diversion from the music that made Wilde popular and from the other artistic directions he's pursued, *Diversions* remains an unjustifiably overlooked album. Considering that much worse material from the same period has been re-released and retrospectively celebrated, a formal reissue of *Diversions* is long overdue, so that a new generation of listeners can appreciate its scope and brilliance.

Neanderthal Man
Hotlegs
1970

Like cockroaches, and maybe Keith Richards, novelty songs are eternal. Every era in musical history has at some point been lionized by pundits for achieving new heights of artistic and aesthetic brilliance – but, inevitably, lurking on the charts at the same time is that era's equivalent of 'I'm Going to Bring A Watermelon to My Girl Tonight' or 'Purple People Eater'. Some pundits will also happily debate for hours what constitutes a novelty song. Is it a one-hit wonder? Is it something that's just outright silly? Is it something catchy but insubstantial? Is it annoying? By all of those definitions, the '70s seemed to be a time that was especially rife with novelty songs – some would even go so far as to argue that disco music was no more than overhyped novelty music. Disco also inspired the appalling 'Disco Duck' which pretty much everyone would agree is a hallmark (or a nadir) of the novelty music genre.

But some '70s songs that could be categorized as novelty songs, and were intended by their creators to be no more than that, turned out to be more substantive in the sense of leading to other opportunities. 'Neanderthal Man' by Hotlegs had that effect not only for the members of that band, but also for some of the other acts that covered it.

'Neanderthal Man' has a distinctive sound: a stomping bass drum topped by an oddly detached vocal crooning a decidedly simple set of lyrics and a somewhat trippy middle eight. It sounds like a couple of guys mucking around in the studio and making things up as they go along, and that's exactly what happened at Strawberry Studios in Stockport, near Manchester. Strawberry was founded in '67 by two Manchester residents: Peter Tattersall, who had worked with Beatles manager Brian Epstein, and Eric Stewart, who had been part of Wayne Fontana and the Mindbenders. In addition to being a vocalist and guitarist with that band, Stewart had written several of its hits, and when the Mindbenders' career petered out, he found himself with enough cash in hand to support himself while deciding what to do next. Tattersall approached him to invest in the studio, and they became partners in the venture.

The studio was named after Stewart's favourite Beatles song, 'Strawberry Fields Forever', and the naming also followed the fruit-related branding example that the Beatles set with their Apple companies. The Strawberry venture was daring not only in being given an unusual name, but in being located in a region that other studios and record labels had generally ignored. At that time, musicians generally accepted that they had to travel to one of the established recording studios in and around London if they wanted to make a good-sounding record – and some doubters questioned whether there was enough potential business for a professional-quality recording studio in northern England to succeed.

Strawberry's two investors were joined by another Mancunian, Graham Gouldman, who had achieved success as a songwriter for the Yardbirds ('For Your Love', 'Heart Full of Soul') and the Hollies ('Look Through Any Window', 'Bus Stop'). Gouldman had also been the Mindbenders' bassist during the last few months of the band's existence. When Gouldman became involved with Strawberry, he brought along his friends Kevin Godley and Lol Creme, who had just graduated from art school and had been involved with Gouldman on various musical projects. But Gouldman's reputation as a songwriter then came to the attention of Jerry Kasenatz and Jeff Katz, two New York-based producers who, as Super K Productions, specialized in 'bubblegum pop' – what critic Dave Marsh described as "ludicrous, if occasionally transcendent, trash".

K&K, as they were known, persuaded Gouldman to become a staff writer for them, which resulted in Gouldman not only splitting his writing and recording energies between Manchester and the US, but also bringing in a source of regular income for Strawberry. Gouldman roped in Creme, Godley and Stewart to participate in recording sessions for K&K at the studio. These efforts resulted in records released under the names of, among others, the Ohio Express, Crazy Elephant, Silver Fleet, and Fighter Squadron.

Strawberry then began to attract many other clients, both locals and out-of-towners. The increased activity meant that new equipment was regularly coming into the studio, and it needed to be set up and tested. And thus one day Stewart was trying out a new four-track recording deck while Godley was drumming and Creme was singing into the bass drum. (At the time, Gouldman was in New York, trying to extricate himself from his contractual obligations with K&K.) Godley said in a recent interview that he had a vague memory of himself, Creme and Stewart in a London cab, singing something about Neanderthal men and Neanderthal girls, and he believed that was what Creme drew on that day to make up a song on the spot. Creme recounted, "Eric was trying to build up a bass drum sound and I was singing, and after three or four tracks of drums, we almost had the whole thing together."

But the track remained a work in progress until Dick Leahy, a staffer at Philips Records, visited Strawberry, and Stewart demonstrated the studio's sound by playing him the track. Leahy told them, "That's a smash", and offered to release the record if the band finished the song. Stewart wrote a middle part, the trio christened themselves Hotlegs after a nickname they had given to Strawberry's lovely receptionist, and 'Neanderthal Man' suddenly became a thing – reaching #2 in the UK and #22 in the US, and charting in several European countries. A promotional video showed Creme, Stewart and Godley performing the song in the studio, interspersed with shots of fur-bikinied dancing ladies doing some sort of odd prehistoric version of the Hitchhike.

'Neanderthal Man' was promptly pounced upon by the musical sub-industry that churned out cut-price albums and EPs with anonymous renditions of current hit songs. Although the arrangements and sounds of these records closely resembled the originals, the record covers only listed the song titles – a clever marketing ploy designed to catch the eye of buyers who knew the name of the song they were looking for, but couldn't remember or didn't know the name of the act. The process of creating these records provided steady work for a host of studio musicians and vocalists, and 'Neanderthal Man' must have been particularly attractive as a potential cover because of its relatively simple structure.

There appear to be two cut-price covers of 'Neanderthal Man'. One was on Volume 12 of *Top of The Pops*, a series of releases on the budget Pickwick Records label that took advantage of the fact that the BBC had apparently neglected to trademark the name of its weekly music-chart show. A YouTube post of Pickwick's 'Neanderthal Man' credits the vocals to Martin Jay, a regular on these anonymous-cover-version sessions who later was part of the disco act 5000 Volts and then worked with Tight Fit and Enigma. The other cut-price cover, on Deacon Records, featured a young Elton John.

John was a pop music fanatic from a young age. He avidly followed the progress of songs up and down the charts, as well as buying as many records as he could and storing them on his bedroom shelves in categories separated by section dividers. When he started to build his own career as a musician, he made regular appearances as a backing vocalist and keyboard player on other acts' recordings, and he also developed a considerable body of work as an anonymous cover artist. According to biographer Philip Norman, "during late 1969 and early 1970, his talent for mimicry earned him at least as much as his true persona". The version of 'Neanderthal Man' featuring John's vocals appeared on Volume 2 of Deacon's *Top of the Pops* EP series and on Volume 4 of Deacon's LP series *Pick of the Pops* (nothing like getting your money's worth). Hilariously, Pickwick Records was unamused by Deacon Records using the same title Pickwick had pinched from the BBC, and sued Deacon for copyright infringement. The lawsuit eventually led to the demise of Deacon's cut-price releases.

It's tempting to imagine John gritting his teeth in the studio, plowing through yet another Top 40 cover version to pay the rent while dreaming of his own future un-anonymous success. However, it has been pointed out that in late 1970, when these records would have been made, John had already released two albums and several singles under his own name; while none had been huge successes, he was starting to get the critical buzz that boosted his reputation prior to his big commercial breakthrough in '71 with 'Your Song'. So while money may have played a part in John's decision to continue working as an anonymous cover artist, it's also entirely possible that he did so simply because he enjoyed the process of recording and the challenge of creating a credible cover. (Anyone interested in hearing more from this phase of his career is encouraged to find the '94 compilation *Reg Dwight's Piano Goes Pop*.)

But meanwhile, what of the song's originators? In retrospect, Godley admitted, "we were a bit big-headed." Hotlegs' members celebrated the success of 'Neanderthal Man' by going on holiday to Barbados for several months. In the fall of '70, with the addition of Gouldman on bass, the band embarked on a UK tour as the opening act for the Moody Blues. However, the tour was cut short after only four dates when the Moodies' bass player John Lodge fell ill. By the time the band got around to recording a complete album, nearly a year had passed since 'Neanderthal Man' had graced the charts. *Hotlegs Thinks School Stinks* was well-received by critics, but the delay between the single's time on the charts and the album's release meant that the album did not sell as well as expected. (It did, however, receive a sort of further recognition when Alice Cooper apparently liked the cover so much that he copied it almost identically for his own '72 album *School's Out*.) A second single, 'Lady Sadie', was so radically different in style from 'Neanderthal Man' that it was not able to attract additional attention. Philips re-released the Hotlegs album under the title *Song*, but the re-release did not spark any renewal of interest.

While Hotlegs's career was starting to slide downhill, an additional cover version of 'Neanderthal Man' came along from the Idle Race, who had initially drawn attention because of the clever songwriting of leader Jeff Lynne and the group's energetic live performances. However, Lynne left the Idle Race in mid-'70 to join his friend Roy Wood in the Move, with the understanding that they would jointly work on another project, which eventually morphed into the Electric Light Orchestra. 'Neanderthal Man' was one of two covers in '70 by the post-Lynne Idle Race, the other being Mungo Jerry's 'In the Summertime'. 'Neanderthal Man', sadly, became the Idle Race's second to last single, and the group disbanded in '72. More memorable covers – "memorable" in both good and bad ways - were by the German duo Adam & Eve, also in '70, and the James Last Orchestra in '71. Both of these used alternating male and female vocalists to turn the song into a Paleolithic love duet.

The former members of Hotlegs, with the full-time addition of Gouldman, eventually retreated back to Strawberry and resumed their sonic experiments. In between working on projects for clients such as Neil Sedaka, Creme, Godley, Stewart, and Gouldman continued creating music for themselves. Producer Jonathan King (no stranger to novelty records himself) heard one of the quartet's songs, "Donna", renamed them as 10cc, signed them to his label, and….things just went from there. 10cc became one of the most successful and creatively adventurous bands of the '70s, and were so popular that in '76 the Philips label tried to get some mileage out of 10cc's success by refurbishing Hotlegs' lone album with a few extra tracks and re-releasing it as *You Didn't Like It Because You Didn't Think of It*. The re-release was greeted with the same indifference as the earlier versions, and thus 'Neanderthal Man' remains the main legacy of Hotlegs' brief existence. But while it may have been a fluke of recording tomfoolery, and continues to irritate some listeners even to this day, 'Neanderthal Man' deserves respect because of its part in leading to some truly astounding music later on.

Lovin' You Ain't Easy
Michel Pagliaro
1971

It is a rare beast indeed that gets nothing but love in YouTube's comments sections, which are generally the habitat of venom-spewing trolls and random nastiness. Michel Pagliaro's 'Lovin' You Ain't Easy' is in the very small category of receiving unanimous YouTube positivity, because pretty much everyone who hears the song falls in love with it. When it was released in '71, it received glowing reviews. Power-pop guru Greg Shaw described it as "a breathtaking performance, brilliant production, and an unforgettable melody supported by crashing open chords worthy of The Who." It has fans all over the world. In the words of one

YouTube commenter, "I consider this to be the best pop song ever. This thing has the highest hooks-per-measure I have ever heard."

'Lovin' You Ain't Easy' had a respectable level of success, being released internationally and charting in the UK and Canada. But understanding the song's cultural and musical context helps to explain why even that level of accomplishment was a remarkable achievement. It also sheds some light on why Pagliaro is simultaneously a one-hit wonder (well, one-and-a-bit) *and* an artist revered for his lengthy career and consistently visionary music.

Pagliaro – "Pag" to his fans - is from Québec, and he holds the distinction of being one of a very few musicians to have both English- and French-language gold-certified hit records in Canada. (A gold hit single in Canada has sold at least 40,000 units.) The fact that this happens so rarely demonstrates the linguistic and cultural challenges faced by Québecois musicians. Nearly all of Québec's residents have French as a first or second language, and Québec is officially a French-language province. As such, Québec has a difficult and different relationship with the rest of Canada; while French and English are Canada's two national official languages, English is the dominant language in most of the country. It would take several long pages of description to fully explore the nuances of these "two solitudes", but to understand the Québec music scene, it's important to know that many Québecois associate the English language and Anglophone culture with a long history of colonialism and oppression of Francophones and of Québec. There is also a strong element within Québec society that regards Québec not as a Canadian province but as a nation within a nation, and also believes the protection and promotion of the French language are important to maintain a distinctive cultural identity for Québec.

Because of these linguistic and cultural tensions, Québecois musicians face a somewhat politicized decision in choosing to perform in French, in English, or in both. Performing in French gives an artist access to a thriving Francophone music industry in Canada, but that industry exists almost solely within Québec. A Canadian from outside Québec who goes into a music store in Montreal or Québec City is usually utterly shocked to see numerous records by artists who sell hundreds of thousands of albums and who tour extensively, but who are almost completely unknown in

English-speaking Canada. Francophone performers from Québec could theoretically find audiences in other French-speaking regions around the world, but Québecois French, and other forms of Canadian French such as Acadian, are often perceived as not being "correct" French, and thus may be disdained elsewhere.

Performing in English can greatly broaden a Québecois artist's potential audience, but that choice can be viewed by Québec nationalists as selling out to Anglo domination – particularly when, as in the case of artists such as the young Celine Dion, the artist does not speak English fluently or has already been successful as a Francophone performer. It's also difficult to convey the depth of negative reactions in some parts of Québec society when popular Francophone music is adapted into English. For example, there was great dismay when the melody of Gilles Vigneault's song 'Mon Pays', considered an unofficial anthem of Québec nationalism, was used by Patsy Gallant (herself a Francophone from New Brunswick) for the '76 English-language disco hit 'From New York to LA'.

Complicating this situation even further is that for much of the 1960s and 1970s, and even to some extent today, the Canadian music industry as a whole was dominated by American- or international-owned interests, who were more concerned with making money rather than with supporting a homegrown Canadian musical scene.

Like many Québec artists of his generation, Pagliaro got his start in the '60s Québec yé-yé scene. While Québec yé-yé featured female stars that resembled the mini-skirted darlings of European yé-yé fame, its more common form was similarly-dressed groups of young men who, with varying degrees of competency, cranked out French-language versions of the Top 40 hits of the day. Pagliaro was part of Les Stringmen, Les Bluebirds, Les Merseys, and finally Les Chanceliers, the latter of which recorded several singles and an album including some original tunes. Pagliaro went solo in '67, at the tender age of 20, and while he continued to record French translations of English-language hits such as 'Hey Jude' and 'Sunny', he also found success with French-language tracks such as 'Comme d'habitude' (originally recorded by French vocalist Claude

François), which was later adapted into English by fellow Montrealer Paul Anka as 'My Way'.

Untangling the chronology of Pagliaro's solo discography is complicated, because his French- and English-language releases were on different labels but often released around the same time. And to make things even more confusing, he recorded no fewer than four different albums that were each at some point released under the title *Pagliaro*. 'Lovin' You Ain't Easy' first appeared on a '72 English-language album titled *Pagliaro* that was later reissued under the title *Rainshowers*.

MUCH Records, the label that released the '72 *Pagliaro*, has its own interesting back story that demonstrates some of the other complexities of the Canadian music industry. Not to be confused with MuchMusic, the '80s TV channel that was the Canadian equivalent of MTV, MUCH was formed in the early '70s. It began as a partnership between Allan Slaight, the president of the CHUM chain of radio stations, and Brian Chater, a UK expat and music industry executive. MUCH was one of the first independent Canadian record labels, and Pagliaro was MUCH's first signing. When MUCH was launched, other Canadian record companies immediately objected to its operations, alleging that MUCH's association with CHUM would give the label's artists an unfair advantage in obtaining radio airplay and promotion. Slaight denied that charge, telling *Billboard* magazine that Pagliaro's first single for the label, 'Give Us One More Chance', "was played on CHUM for two weeks and then dropped because of lack of response" and was only added back onto the chain's playlists once it became a national hit through airplay on other stations.

Pagliaro recorded 'Lovin' You Ain't Easy' sometime in '71 at Apple Studios in London, allegedly in between session times booked by Badfinger. Some sources say that the recording sessions were in Abbey Road Studios – a confusion that may have occurred because the record's engineer, John Mills, worked at both Abbey Road and Apple. But Pagliaro himself told an interviewer in 2017 that he used the Beatles' own Apple studio: "People always think of Abbey Road Studios at the crosswalk with the four Beatles, but Apple Studios, I always remember that street number, 3 Savile Row was the building where Apple Corps was. The Beatles had installed a studio in the basement. The top of the building where we recorded is where the Beatles had their final public performance on the rooftop. For me it was just another studio that had some cool vibes in the recording room."

'Lovin' You Ain't Easy' was released in late '71 as the first single from *Pagliaro* a/k/a *Rainshowers*. The song was released on Pye in the UK (possibly due to Chater's connections in the music industry there), as well as in the US, most of Europe, and Japan. This level of international exposure was extremely uncommon for a Canadian pop musician at that time, especially for a relative unknown. The brief appearance of 'Lovin' You Ain't Easy' on the UK charts, where it topped out at #31, scored Pagliaro an appearance on the BBC's *Top of the Pops* TV show in January '72. 'Some Sing, Some Dance' was the second single from the album, and while it did not have chart success outside Canada, both it and 'Lovin' You Ain't Easy' were chosen by Greg Shaw in '78 for inclusion in his list of "All-Time Power Pop Records" in *BOMP!* magazine. Astoundingly, while 'Rainshowers' has been covered by several artists, there don't appear to be any recorded covers of either 'Lovin' You Ain't Easy' or 'Some Sing, Some Dance'. So get with it, any power-pop bands or musicians reading this - here are two fantastic songs just waiting for you.

Another factor may or may not have affected Pagliaro's success, depending on who you ask. In '72, Canada's federal government implemented a policy designed to support Canadian performers against the domination of US interests in recording and broadcasting. The "Cancon" (Canadian content) rules required radio stations to devote 30% of their programming to releases composed or performed by Canadian artists. 'Lovin' You Ain't Easy' clearly met those criteria, as Pagliaro was Canadian and was the song's co-writer as well as its performer. But 'Lovin' You Ain't Easy' may not have benefited from the new rules, because the first year or so after Cancon's implementation was marked by a lot of confusion. Radio programmers struggled to figure out how to follow the new directives; for example, did a song qualify as Cancon if it was co-written by a Canadian and a non-Canadian? Many fine releases by Canadian artists may have been overlooked as potential Cancon qualifiers, or just as great radio-friendly songs, because of the unclear criteria and the radio stations' struggle to meet the new requirements.

While having success with English-language songs, Pagliaro also maintained his French-language recording career. In '72 he wrote and recorded 'J'entends frapper', a hard-rocking tune which is well worth a listen even for non-French speakers. 'J'entends frapper' was a hit in Francophone Canada at the same time that 'Some Sing, Some Dance' was a hit in Anglophone Canada, which, as far as anyone can tell, makes Pagliaro the only artist to have had simultaneous hit singles on the French- and English-language Canadian charts. The respect for 'J'entends frapper' is such that the song was subsequently inducted into the Canadian Songwriters' Hall of Fame.

Pagliaro had another Canadian English-language hit in '75 with 'What the Hell I Got', but then his interests seemed to shift more toward writing and recording mostly in French. He continued to record original songs in English, but many of his subsequent English-language tracks were covers of classic rock and roll hits, albeit very passionate and convincing covers. He also stopped releasing albums regularly, and worked mainly on musical projects that took his fancy, without being locked into the commercial expectation of frequent recording and touring. As one writer put it, "At one time, it was believed that Michel Pagliaro would become an international rock star. Then he disappeared, long enough to become a true artist." His French- and English-language recordings have been re-released on several compilations – including a massive 13-CD box set, *Tonnes de Flashs*, in 2011 - and there are also several DVDs of his live performances. So there's plenty of great viewing or listening out there for anyone who wants to hear more from this extraordinarily talented musician.

In 2008, Pagliaro was presented with the Governor-General of Canada's Lifetime Achievement Award for Artistic Achievement in Popular Music; in 2017, he donated his personal musical archives, which chronicle his career from 1961 to 2016, to the National Archives of Canada. He currently performs gigs at music festivals in Quebec and elsewhere in Canada, and recently embarked on a series of acoustic-only solo shows. He's also been a mentor on *La Voix*, the Québec version of *The Voice* talent search TV show, working with the "team" of fellow Québecois rocker Éric Lapointe. Pagliaro may now be less well known to English-speaking audiences, beyond the rapturous affection that 'Lovin' You Ain't Easy', continues to inspire, but he is still recognized as "the face of Québec rock" - a legendary and highly-respected figure in the French-language music scene. And he has no intentions of slowing down. He told an interviewer in 2017, "I'm just happy that I keep doing what I love to do, and I try to do it as much as I can."

Everything Stops for Tea
Long John Baldry
1972

Most music fans outside the UK know Long John Baldry mostly as a sort of mystical godfather of the early '60s British blues scene. At different times, his bands included young Rod Stewart and young Elton John, and both credit him with mentoring them in the early part of their careers. Indeed, when Reginald Dwight chose his stage name, he chose the surname "John" as a tribute to his friend ("Elton" came from saxophonist Elton Dean). But what gets lost in that mythology, especially for non-UK fans, is that Baldry's four major UK chart hits in the 60s were not in the blues and soul style that he was renowned for – they were decidedly mainstream Top 40 fluff. And that, in turn, led to the career stagnation which 'Everything Stops for Tea' was perhaps intended to correct.

As a vocalist in the early '60s, Baldry toured extensively and collaborated with some of the most high-profile names in British blues, such as Cyril Davies and Alexis Korner. However, his records went in a musical direction almost directly opposite to that of his live performances, and that was not entirely by chance. According to biographer Paul Myers, Baldry was jealous of fellow musicians such as Georgie Fame who had used hit pop singles to build a commercial reputation while continuing to be respected by their peers on the R&B/blues circuit; he wanted that same kind of success for himself. In search of that goal, Baldry signed to United Records, which released two albums – '64's *Long John's Blues* and the more pop-oriented *Looking at Long John* in '66 – and seven singles, but none of these made any significant impact on the charts. A frustrated Baldry left United in '67 and signed with Pye Records, where he was teamed with producer and songwriter Tony Macauley. Macauley had recently brought The Foundations to stardom with the catchy 'Build Me Up Buttercup', and admitted that he was surprised to hear that a blues artist like Baldry wanted to record more mainstream material. Nevertheless, he agreed to take on the task.

Macauley pitched Baldry a song with the weepy title 'Let the Heartaches Begin', which he had written a few years previously but hadn't been able to match with the right performer. Baldry agreed to record the song, but the process of doing so turned out to be a learning experience for both. Pye sprung for the cost of a studio orchestra to play on the session, but Macauley had never worked with a live orchestra before. Additionally, Baldry, used to the improvisation and spontaneity of live performance, was not accustomed to singing a song at the exact tempo in which it was written. Despite those challenges, 'Let the Heartaches Begin' became a #1 hit, followed in quick succession by three other Top 30 entries: 'When the Sun Comes Shinin' Through', 'Mexico', and 'It's Too Late Now'.

The subsequent course of Baldrey's career, however, might be characterized as proving the truth of the statement 'be careful what you wish for'. Thanks to his chart successes, Baldry was able to command top fees for playing at cabarets and clubs. But audiences in those venues expected to hear songs like 'Heartaches', not the blues-oriented numbers that dominated the repertoire of Baldry and his band Bluesology. 'Heartaches' stood out in the set like a sore thumb, and the members of Bluesology could often be caught making faces and mocking the song while they played it. To add insult to injury, many of the fans that loved Baldry's earlier work were appalled at what they saw as a crass sell-out for the sole purpose of making money, and shunned both his records and his performances.

A promised trip to the US might have exposed Baldry to wider acceptance, but the trip was cancelled after 'Mexico' became a larger UK hit than expected, thanks to its being extensively played on UK television to accompany coverage of the 1968 Summer Olympics. Baldry's management and record company elected to have him stay in the UK and go on tour on the back of 'Mexico''s popularity, but Baldry's performances on that tour were less than enthusiastic; he later said that 'Mexico' was such a horrible song that he never wanted to hear or sing it again. Baldry's reputation for partying and drinking, along with his not-so-secret homosexuality, also contributed to the decline of his career. By the end of the '60s, he fit into neither the pop world nor the blues world, and was sliding even more deeply into aimlessness and substance abuse.

By the early '70s, both John and Stewart had found solo success, and, as John told Myers, they felt that they could "turn around and do something for someone who had treated us so kindly and was such a great man to work for". John and Stewart agreed to produce one side each of an album for Baldry, and Stewart arranged for Baldry to be signed to the Warner Brothers label in the US – a deal which some suggested was perhaps motivated not by any interest the label might have had in Baldry, but more by the label wanting to get its hands on the Faces, who had the same manager as Stewart. Nevertheless, John and Stewart proceeded with the recording project; they booked separate blocks of session time at different studios, and each worked with Baldry on their own when they were available. Both also involved Baldry in choosing songs for the album, which resulted in a fascinating mix of styles that showed off Baldry's interpretive versatility and strong baritone voice. The resulting record, *It Ain't Easy*, was very positively received, and contained several rootsy, passionate performances, particularly Baldry's duets with Maggie Bell on Leadbelly's 'Black Girl' and on the title track.

It Ain't Easy was successful enough for Warner Brothers to book Baldry on a US tour, as the opening act on a bill starring Savoy Brown and Fleetwood Mac; the company also undertook a North American re-release of the *Long John's Blues* album. Baldry was a hit with US audiences who knew little or nothing about him, but there were numerous reports from the road about his problematic drinking, which was excessive even by the wild standards of rock and roll tours. Nevertheless, Warner Brothers was confident enough that lightning would strike twice that it agreed to fund the production of another Baldry album co-produced by John and Stewart.

'Everything Stops for Tea', which became the album's title track, was the first track on Stewart's half of that second album. Stewart told Myers that he suggested the song because "I loved it when John sang all that stuff, so I said, 'Why don't you try it on the album?'. And he did a marvellous job of it." In selecting a song from the '30s, Stewart and Baldry were also tapping into a renewed contemporary interest in theatrical-sounding songs – not only originals, such as those that the Bonzo Dog Doo-Dah Band found on 78-rpm discs in second-hand shops and then added to their own repertoire, but also pastiches such as the Beatles' 'Being for the Benefit of Mr. Kite'.

While Stewart identifies 'Everything Stops for Tea' as a "Noel Coward song", the song was actually co-written by three musical-theatre veterans and debuted in the '37 film musical *Come Out of The Pantry* – a musical which itself had a rather convoluted history. The film was based on a '21 stage play which had first been made into a silent film, then into the musical film *Honey*, and then into the '37 musical film with entirely new songs, including 'Everything Stops for Tea'. The film's plot involved a financially strapped English nobleman who takes a job as a footman in an American millionaire's mansion, and falls in love with the millionaire's daughter. The star of the movie, Jack Buchanan, recorded 'Everything Stops for Tea' as a single, and it was covered by several dance bands and soloists in the '30s and '40s. But save for a version by actress/singer Tsai Chin in '65, the song seems to have gone largely unnoticed until Baldry and Stewart tackled it.

The arrangement of Baldry's version closely follows Buchanan's arrangement, with a brief spoken-word playlet opening the song. Baldry was legendary among his friends for his skills as a raconteur, and he had already demonstrated his storytelling skills on the first track of *It Ain't Easy*. On the spoken-word introduction of that song, he recounted being arrested in '56 while busking in London, and being brought before a judge who heard testimony about his "boujie-woujie music" – leading into the explosive 'Don't Try to Lay No Boogie-Woogie on the King of Rock and Roll'. ' Everything Stops For Tea' begins with a chaotic dialogue between an overwrought Baldry, a harassing fan, and an itinerant songwriter, after which Baldry is served with a calming cuppa – and then smoothly slides into the song's buoyant melody, set to the lilt of a string orchestra.

The critical consensus on *Everything Stops For Tea* was that for all its strong moments – the title track, 'Come Back Again', and 'Mother Ain't Dead' among them – it was a somewhat lackluster effort. Despite John and Stewart repeating their roles as producers, participation by many of the same musicians, and even using the same two recording studios, *Everything Stops for Tea* didn't have the same spirit and energy as *It Ain't Easy*. John and Stewart's increasingly busy careers meant that they were not consistently present for the recording sessions; Stewart told Myers that he was only able to work on "two or three tracks", although he is credited with producing all six tracks on Side 2 of the album. The *Rolling Stone* review of *Everything Stops for Tea* dismissed Baldry as "tak[ing] good songs from real artists and divert[ing] attention from them with his lifeless copies" (ouch) and suggested that "if they had as much taste as they apparently do loyalty, Stewart and John could do us all a big favor by lending their names to some of the really brilliant English comeback artists, such as Phillip Goodhand-Tait, who are being shamefully overlooked." Baldry himself told a reporter that *Everything Stops for Tea* was "a good album, but not a great album. It's still my ambition to make a great album."

'Everything Stops for Tea' was released as a single, as was 'Iko Iko', but the album itself barely charted in the US, and Warner Brothers ended its contract with Baldry. Baldry then moved on to collaborate with producer Jimmy Horowitz. Horowitz had worked on both of the Warner Brothers albums, so he understood Baldry's musical strengths. However, while Baldry had already demonstrated that commercialism was not his driving artistic motivation, both of his albums with Horowitz included so many different styles of songs that there might not been enough material in any one style to appeal to fans of that genre. Both albums also suffered, perhaps unfairly, from being significantly out of step with what was dominating the charts when they were released. '73's *Good to Be Alive*, which was originally released only in the UK, went almost unnoticed in the wake of glam rock; Baldry then signed to Casablanca Records in the US, which released *Good to Be Alive* and '75's *Welcome to Club Casablanca*, the latter of which was largely ignored because it wasn't a disco record.

Baldry's despair about his career troubles was increasingly manifested in drinking and unreliability, and his situation was certainly not helped by a series of questionable management deals. His mounting problems eventually resulted in him attempting suicide by an overdose of drugs, which led to him being committed to a mental hospital. His experiences there, though, led to his career being rejuvenated with the *Baldry's Out* album in '79, which, in addition to the confessional title track, gave him a hit with his duet with Kathi McDonald on 'You've Lost That Lovin' Feeling'.

Baldry moved permanently to Canada in the '80s, and in between touring and recording a series of folk/blues albums for the Stony Plain label, he developed a secondary career as a voiceover artist for animation and video games. Sadly, in 2005 he died at the age of 64 of a lung infection. 'Everything Stops for Tea', meanwhile, has been taken up by revivalist swing/dance bands such as the Pasadena Roof Orchestra and Graham Dalby & The London Swing Orchestra, and, most recently, by the genre-mixing "gentleman rapper" Professor Eccentric. But Baldry's version still stands as a charming reminder of the power of collaboration, and of the generosity of two successful musicians supporting a friend who helped them on their way.

You Put Something Better Inside Me
Stealers Wheel
1972

Gerry Rafferty's career encompassed both tremendous achievement and enormous sadness. He was involved with two huge hit singles – Stealers Wheel's 'Stuck in the Middle with You' and his own 'Baker Street' – which made him richer and more commercially successful than many of his peers. But he was also a quiet and reclusive soul who actively resisted the conventions associated with musical stardom. He once said, "My life doesn't stand or fall by the amount of people who buy my records." His life ended tragically after years of struggling with alcoholism and mental illness – which makes the thankfulness expressed in 'You Put Something Better Inside Me' even more poignant.

'Better' first appeared on Stealers Wheel's '72 debut self-titled album, as one of four tracks co-written by Rafferty and Joe Egan. Rafferty and Egan both grew up in the Scottish city of Paisley, and met in their late teens as members of amateur bands that played clubs and dances on weekends. Rafferty recounted that he "really started writing when I was 17. When I first heard Lennon and McCartney I thought it was magic. It was after that that I first started writing songs on my own, and then when I met Joe we started writing songs together as well as individually." In addition to being in several bands together, Egan and Rafferty also recorded a single during a brief stint with the short-lived The Fifth Column.

Rafferty's and Egan's paths diverged when Rafferty met Billy Connolly and was invited to join Connolly's group the Humblebums. Rafferty and Connolly made two albums together, and the contrast of a loud, comedic extrovert with a self-described "uptight, shy introvert" made for an engaging on-stage chemistry. But Rafferty was clearly the serious songwriter in the Humblebums – "I never reckoned Billy's songs and nor did he; he never took them that seriously either, but he wrote them and they filled up five or ten minutes" – and that imbalance was obvious in their recorded work. Hiring a backing band to fill out the band's sound in concert didn't resolve the problem, and the duo amicably split up in '71. However, contractual obligations meant that the Humblebums still owed their record label one more album, which led to Rafferty making the solo album *Can I Have My Money Back?* He invited Egan to work on that album with him, which brought them back together professionally and led to the start of Stealers Wheel.

At that time, Rafferty had been happily married for two years to his wife Carla, and they had already become the parents of a daughter, Martha. Rafferty's friends and associates say that his songs were always based on his real-life experiences and feelings, and while it's not clear what Egan and Rafferty individually contributed to writing 'Better', the simple declaration of appreciation could well be Rafferty's expression of gratitude to his wife and child. The stately melody and chords of the song might also have been influenced by the folk songs and hymns that the younger Rafferty sang in three-part harmony with his brothers.

Stealers Wheel were signed to A&M Records in '72, and American songwriters and producers Jerry Leiber and Mike Stoller were hired to produce the band's debut abum. While most of the band's members were thrilled to work with the legendary pair – and to do so in the Beatles' Apple Studios - Rafferty was suspicious of the duo's history of hits and whether that meant Stealers Wheel would be forced into being "commercial". Leiber and Stoller thought that the arrangements of the band's songs were fairly basic, and felt that they could, in Stoller's words, "enhance that with some of our ideas, to add a flavour that it didn't have to begin with." In their autobiography, Leiber and Stoller claimed that working on the project was "a blast" and described the band as "open-minded [and] open-hearted", but in a later interview, Stoller admitted that "it took a long time" to reach consensus on artistic directions because of Rafferty's stubbornness.

Stealers Wheel's self-titled album including 'Better' was released in '72. 'Better' perhaps sounds a little cluttered because of the multiple vocal harmonies and interjections, but on other tracks, Leiber and Stoller's "flavours", such as the slippery slide guitar and the handclaps on 'Stuck in the Middle With You', elevate something good to something great. But not long after *Stealers Wheel* was released, Rafferty quit the band; Egan said Rafferty never told him why. Stealers Wheel carried on with Egan as the front man, which meant, among other things, that when 'Stuck' became a major hit in the US and the UK in '73, Egan had to mime Rafferty's lead vocal in the promotional video.

The band persuaded Rafferty to rejoin so they could capitalize on the momentum from that hit single, but prior to a performance on the *Top of the Pops* TV show, Rafferty decided that he was fed up with "feeling rushed" through rehearsals, promotional appearances, and concert dates; immediately after the broadcast ended, he quit again. He came back long enough to complete Stealers Wheel's second album, *Ferguslie Park*. Perhaps recognizing the comparative weakness of that album, A&M released 'Better' as a single backed by the *Ferguslie Park* track 'Wheelin'', but although 'Star' was a middling hit, after a third album the band was done for good. The subsequent legal and contractual fallout lasted nearly three years, and required Rafferty to regularly travel from Glasgow to London to meet with lawyers and accountants. After a day of business in London he would regularly head off to visit a friend who lived near Baker Street....but that's another story about another song.

When 'Better' came out in '72, Kiki Dee was also an artist who was struggling with the uncertainties of the music business. She had released two well-reviewed albums, one in the UK and one in the US, and was one of a very few British artists that had been signed to Motown Records. But neither album had been successful, and she had left the US to return to the UK. She worked as a singer of cover versions of hit songs on TV and radio, and also made ends meet as a backup singer on other artists' recording sessions. However, this was also the time when Elton John's career was rapidly ascending to stratospheric heights, and the resulting financial windfall meant that he could fulfill his long-held dream of owning his own record company. As shown by the work he did with Long John Baldry (see this book's chapter on 'Everything Stops for Tea'), John was more than happy to use his own reputation and resources to support artists that he liked and that he felt deserved more attention. Thus, when Rocket Records came into being, Dee was one of his first signings.

Dee released four albums on Rocket. The ones that got the most attention were '73's *I've Got the Music in Me* (thanks to the hit title song) and '77's *Kiki Dee*, which contained the mega hit duet with John, 'Don't Go Breaking My Heart'. However, her first Rocket album, *Loving and Free*, is exceptional, perhaps the best of the lot. It has an adventurous range of material, which is admirable in giving Dee the chance to show off her strong, throaty voice and her ability to convincingly handle nearly any style of music. Her version of 'Better' on *Loving and Free* highlights the wonderful tones of her voice and, with the backing harmonies on the chorus, also brings out the gospel undertones in the song.

Speaking of gospel, another cover version of 'Better' that same year was by Ted Neeley, who was on a roll from playing the title role in *Jesus Christ Superstar* on stage and on film. Neeley was an experienced musical theatre performer, but he had also had a recording career as far back as '66, when he fronted the Teddy Neeley Band for their one album, along with releasing several solo singles. His musical style has been described as "southern rock" and his version of 'Better' on *Ted Neeley 1974 A.D.* follows that path, with his slightly raspy voice making him sound very much like someone who could use something better in his life.

Elton John's pal Rod Stewart recorded 'Better' in '74, as part of the sessions for his *Smiler* album. It would be kind to say that *Smiler* received mixed reviews, as it seemed to embody Stewart torn between the type of music he loved, the pressure to sustain his success, and the desire to have a good time. 'Better' was not included on *Smiler*'s running order, and while the album has its bright spots, it also has a lot of dreck ('Let Me Be Your Car', anyone?), which makes the listener wonder how 'Better' would have fared amidst such extremes. 'Better' was finally released on an anthology in '96, and it's stunning; Stewart's vocals are perfectly melded with the duet vocal from Irene Chanter (who also sang backup on Dee's version) and this could easily stand with the best work from Stewart's earlier career. In '75, Roger Daltrey recorded a rather by-the-numbers version of 'Better' during the sessions for his solo album *Ride a Rock Horse*; this version was later released as a B-side to his '77 single 'One of the Boys' and was later anthologized on the US and European *Best Bits* compilation.

Raphael Ravenscroft, who played the memorable saxophone riff on 'Baker Street', capitalized on that moment of glory by getting a solo album deal in '79. According to one source, Portrait Records, a subsidiary of Epic Records in the US, was flush with cash after the unexpected mid-'80s success of their act Heart, and some of that bonanza was funnelled into new signings. Ravenscroft was obviously a skilled musician, but it may have been too much to expect him to carry an album on his own. *Her Father Didn't Like Me Anyway* (the title came from another Rafferty song on the album) has never been re-released, and the audio of only two tracks has been uploaded to YouTube. But the sleazy album cover showing Ravenscroft, his saxophone, and a lingerie-clad babe in a bedroom - plus the lounge-lizard feel of the album tracks posted online - indicate that his version of 'Better' would probably not be, well, better.

Rafferty comes back into the story of 'Better' in 2000, when he recorded a solo version on his final studio album, *Another World*. The worldwide success of 'Baker Street' by some accounts earned him £80,000 each year in royalties. While he had some smaller hits later in the '80s, his record sales declined and he refused to do what the music business expected a musician with a hit to do; for example, he never toured in the US even after 'Baker Street' was a smash there. The steady flow of revenue from 'Baker Street' allowed him to work only when he wanted to and on what he wanted. But his longtime co-producer and friend Hugh Murphy passed away in '98, and Rafferty's work seemed less focused after that. Rafferty's vocal on 'Better' is powerful and much more stylistically varied than the gentle croon of his earlier work, and there are beautiful harmonies on the song's chorus. However, the track is very much a product of its time, with washes of glossy synthesizers and a highly polished, almost sterile sound. It may be that without Murphy's influence Rafferty's admitted perfectionism led to the track being made almost too perfect. His recording career ended after another independent release in 2009; he passed away from liver disease in 2011.

Of late, Rafferty's work has sometimes been unfairly slotted into that dreadful musical genre snarkily labeled as 'yacht rock'. His daughter Martha has said, quite rightly, "It was unfortunate that he got labelled as a one-hit, '70s soft-rock artist when he was a lot more than that." Rafferty's work may lack loud guitars and shrieking and pyrotechnics, but that doesn't mean it lacks passion and relevance and meaning – it has all of those and then some. 'You Put Something Better Inside Me' is a beautiful testimony to that.

Sail On Sailor
The Beach Boys
1973

When the Beach Boys recorded 'Sail On Sailor', there could not have been a better metaphor than the sailor to characterize the band and its circumstances. The group was facing the possibility that some of its key members might no longer participate, and it had relocated to another continent in search of new artistic directions. In that context, 'Sail On Sailor' stands as a bold declaration of determination in the face of turbulence. And, like all great seafaring sagas, the story of 'Sail On Sailor' itself is full of improbable characters and unexpected occurrences.

'Sail On Sailor' has five credited co-authors: Brian Wilson, Tandyn Almer, Ray Kennedy, Van Dyke Parks, and Jack Rieley. As is the case with so many events in the Beach Boys' history – a history that has been described as "undying dysfunction" with "ugly lawsuits and squabbling" - the story of how the song originated depends on which version of the story you choose to believe. Danny Hutton of Three Dog Night told Wilson biographer Peter Ames Carlin that Parks and Wilson wrote 'Sail On Sailor' in '71, and "air[ed] it out at his house", with Almer (composer of the Association's 'Along Comes Mary') and Kennedy adding their contributions "eventually".

However, in a 2005 interview, Kennedy claimed that Hutton called him over to his house in 1970 because Three Dog Night "needed a hit" and "stuck me in [a] room with Brian for three days" to create the song. In Kennedy's words, "We went in and cut the basic tracks with Three Dog Night; we hadn't slept in about a week. Then Brian got up with a razor blade and cut the tapes and said, 'Only Ray Kennedy or Van Dyke Parks can do this song.' And he left. We all stood there looking at each other going, 'What?'" Former Beach Boys studio engineer Stephen Desper has stated that some of the band recorded a demo of 'Sail On Sailor' in '71; writer Brian Chidester, who was allowed access to some of the Beach Boys' archives in 2014, indicated that the '71 demo tape existed and had been heard by "several Beach Boys historians". But the demo tape, according to Chidester, was "in the possession of a venerated Beatles collector" who disappeared with it.

In '72, led by Carl Wilson and manager Rieley, the Beach Boys, their families, and their staff moved to Holland. Different sources describe different reasons for the move. Some say that Rieley, who was encouraging the band to become more "topical" and "hip" (a strategy manifested in the '71 album *Surf's Up*), thought that a change of scene would encourage the band's creativity. In one interview, Rieley said that "the boys needed new influences, new sparks, to open stuff up." Others (jokingly, or perhaps not) say that the Netherlands was appealing to the band because recreational drugs were more easily available there than in the US. And some say that since the band had a devoted following in Europe, they felt it would be easier to do lengthy tours around the continent if they were based there; they could also record albums in between tours. Some, all, or none of this may be true, but the latter theory is at least partially supported by the fact that the Beach Boys brought with them the recording studio that was in Brian Wilson's home. At considerable expense to the band, the studio was disassembled into pieces, packed and shipped, and then reassembled in a converted barn in Baambrugge. Wilson himself also joined the group in Holland, although his paranoia of flying meant that he missed several scheduled flights before he actually made the trip across the Atlantic.

The group that assembled in Baambrugge included two new band members: South African guitarist/singer Blondie Chaplin and drummer Ricky Fataar. Carl Wilson had seen Chaplin and Fataar play in London in '68 with their band The Flames, and had signed the band to the Beach Boys' Brother Records label as The Flame (to avoid confusion with James Brown's backing band). Carl produced the band's lone self-titled US album, but after it flopped, Rieley invited Chaplin and Fataar to become Beach Boys – not only because of the new energy they could bring to a group struggling to find its identity, but also so they could fill in as needed for the increasingly unreliable Dennis Wilson and the troubled Brian.

Rieley claimed that after the move "the guys loved the place", but other accounts portray some of the band members and their entourage as homesick and feeling dislocated and isolated. Brian only appeared in the studio occasionally; allegedly, he spent most of his time holed up in his rented house, listening to Randy Newman's album *Sail Away* over and over again. However, both Chaplin and Carl Wilson described a relaxed, informal atmosphere. The band members commuted to the studio, by bicycle or leased Mercedes sedan, from their houses all around the area, and there were regular breaks for lunch at the pub up the road. Chaplin and Fataar were also able to have conversations with the locals using the Dutch that they knew from growing up in South Africa.

Holland, the album that the Beach Boys recorded in Baambrugge, was a definite departure from the band's famous sun-and-sand songs. Tracks such as the three-part 'California Saga',

'The Trader', and 'Steamboat' were longer, more complex, and more adventurous. But when Warner Brothers record executives Mo Ostin and David Berson heard the album, according to Nick Kent in the *New Musical Express*, they "immediately sent it back to the band with a memo to the effect that it wasn't good enough to warrant release in this form".

And here the stories diverge again. One version has Van Dyke Parks, then working a day job at Warner Brothers Records, going to Brian Wilson's house with his new Walkman cassette recorder, intending to get Wilson to write an additional song for *Holland*. The other version – which largely fits Parks' description - is that when Warner Brothers rejected *Holland*, Parks already possessed a cassette tape containing a preliminary version of 'Sail On Sailor', which he had recorded during a previous meeting with Wilson. In this telling, upon hearing of the band's quandary, Parks found the tape and played it for the Warner Brothers executives to show that the band had a salvageable song that could be added to *Holland*.

Parks says he gave the tape with the rough version of 'Sail On Sailor' to Warner Brothers in '72 and never saw it again. But published accounts of the tape's contents describe Parks urging Wilson to "cut the shit and play the tune" and "write a fuckin' middle-eight", and Wilson asking Parks to "convince me I'm not crazy". In between all that, though, there was enough resembling a song to convince Warner Brothers to pay for a further recording session. So the Beach Boys reconvened in the fall of '72 in Los Angeles to record 'Sail On Sailor', with lyrics revised by Rieley.

Carl Wilson sang the lead vocal on the alleged earlier demo of the song, and Dennis Wilson took the lead on a few takes during the '72 session - but Blondie Chaplin sang lead on the version of the song that was released. Chaplin told author Mark Dillon that 'Sail On Sailor' "has so many words to get around to make it flow into the melody, [and] that drove me nuts". But Chaplin's passionate vocal clearly drew on what Dillon describes as "frustrations stewing since his Apartheid-era childhood", and on the stress of constant relocation and travel. Gerry Beckley (from the band America), Billy Hinsche, and Tony Martin Jr. contributed additional backing vocals to the track.

The revised 'Sail On Sailor' was deemed acceptable by Warner Brothers and duly added to *Holland*'s running order. The album was finally released in January '73, by which time most of the band members and their families had moved back to California. Rieley, who remained in Holland, was fired as the Beach Boys' manager, allegedly after the band became aware of the huge amounts of money that had been spent on their European sojourn. 'Sail On Sailor' was released as a single, but was not a success – it only got to #79 in the US charts, and was the B-side of the single 'California/California Saga' which reached #37 in the UK.

The album and the single both received generally positive reviews, being recognized as a step toward musical maturity for the band. But in Chaplin's words, "it wasn't allowed enough time to see what happens." 'Sail on Sailor' was quickly incorporated into the Beach Boys' live shows, but, as one reviewer commented in '75, "'Trader', 'Sail On Sailor' and 'California' are The Boys now, but they have to be shoved into the middle of the set because not enough people pay them attention." For much of the '70s and '80s, 'Sail On Sailor' remained the most recent song in the band's live shows, until the vile 'Kokomo' became a #1 hit in '88.

The next twist in the saga of 'Sail On Sailor' was its first (sort of) cover version. In '75 – the same year that the Beach Boys re-released the song as a single - Ray Kennedy became part of the group KGB, with Mike Bloomfield, Carmine Appice, Barry Goldberg, and Ric Grech. KGB's first album included 'Sail On Sailor', which also became a single - but KGB's version was credited only to Wilson and Kennedy and had completely different lyrics than the Beach Boys' version, chronicling the despair of a "coked-up" gospel singer. KGB's instrumental arrangement of the song was also slower and more bluesy than the swaying, rhythmic Beach Boys arrangement. Kennedy also recorded his version of 'Sail On Sailor' for his '80 solo album.

Covers of the song – the Beach Boys version - have been recorded by, among others, Golden Earring, the Bluetones, Jimmy Buffett, Sting & Lulu, Man, Madeline Bell, and Shawn Colvin. 'Sail On Sailor' has been played in concert by acts as diverse as the Chris Robinson Brotherhood, Susan Cowsill, and Mark Ronson with Sean Lennon. After leaving the Beach Boys in '73, Chaplin also regularly performed the song in his own concerts, and as part of Brian Wilson's touring band.

'Sail On Sailor' has been extensively anthologized in Beach Boys re-releases, including a live version on the '73 *Beach Boys in Concert* album, and was on the soundtrack of the Martin Scorsese film *The Departed*. It's also been included in many "all-star" and "tribute" events featuring Beach Boys and/or Brian Wilson songs. In this format, the song has been performed by, for example, Matthew Sweet and Darius Rucker (the 2001 All-Star Tribute to Brian Wilson), and Boz Scaggs (the 2015 'Brian Fest'). Two renditions of 'Sail On Sailor' from this body of work are particularly notable. In '86 Ray Charles performed an outstanding version of the song at the Beach Boys' 25th anniversary concert; he was introduced by Brian Wilson as "the voice I had in mind when I wrote [the song]– a voice full of soul that only a great gospel singer could possess". And in '96 singer/songwriter Rodney Crowell – a man who knows his way around a good song – recorded 'Sail On Sailor' with the Beach Boys for *Stars and Stripes Vol. 2*, a planned sequel to the band's *Stars and Stripes Vol. 1* album. The sequel was never released as an album, but Crowell's performance is included on the *Stars and Stripes* DVD, and the audio of the track is available on YouTube.

Both Brian Wilson and Mike Love published autobiographies in 2016. Wilson mentions that "coke was around" when he worked on 'Sail On Sailor' but has little else to say about the song. However, Love describes a backstage dispute involving 'Sail On Sailor' during the Beach Boys' 2012 50th anniversary tour. According to Love, Wilson was singing lead on 'Sail On Sailor' during that tour, and Love requested that his daughter Ambha be allowed to sing the song onstage. Love claims that Wilson's wife Melinda complained to Love's wife Jacquelyn that Ambha should be singing one of Love's songs, not one of Wilson's, and that the resulting argument got so heated and personal that Love called the band's management and told them he was quitting the tour. However, he says, they persuaded him that "my pulling out would be extremely disruptive to the whole enterprise" and he decided to stay on.

Since then, Wilson and the Beach Boys have toured separately. And both Wilson and, as one website describes them, "the touring entity that is legally capable of calling itself The Beach Boys" continue to play 'Sail On Sailor' in their live shows. So who knows? In the future, there may be even more chapters to add to the epic tale of this song. Sail on, sailors.

129/Matinee Idyll
Split Enz
1973

Nearly all of the songs in this book have been covered at least once, but the song that's the subject of this chapter – '129'/'Matinee Idyll' by Split Enz – has, as far as I can tell, never been covered. But it's in here because I firmly believe that Split Enz are a hugely underrated band. If you shuddered in the '70s or '80s as they pranced across screen or stage in their outlandish costumes and bizarre hairstyles, you might decide to stop reading right now. But their unique appearance, and the creativity it reflected, was only one part of what made them truly great; the other part was their songs. The songs were heartbreaking, invigorating, mournful, and absurd, and all were presented with an admirable "this is what we do" attitude: not dismissive of their audience, but secure in their distinctive artistic vision. Split Enz' story is full of "if only" turns of fate – as demonstrated by the evolution of the song that is the subject of this chapter - and perhaps, if many things had worked out differently, they might have achieved the acclaim they truly deserve.

Split Enz – or Split Ends, as they first called themselves - came together around '70 through friendships and connections formed at the University of Auckland. The genesis of the group was the creative synergy between Tim Finn, from the rural New Zealand town of Te Awamutu, and Phil Judd, from the seaside region of Hastings. To understand how truly remarkable Split Enz's journey was, think of rural New Zealand in comparison to the urban city of Auckland; then think of the small country of New Zealand in comparison to its much larger neighbour of Australia; and then think of even big Australia's isolation and distance from the rest of the world. To be internationally successful, any band from New Zealand had to, and still has to, move through that geographic progression into unfamiliar, progressively bigger and more competitive markets.

In the past, one or all of those transitions have proved to be too much for many excellent New Zealand bands. But the place where Split Enz started may have allowed them the space for the musical and artistic experimentation that sparked their steadfast self-confidence. Some writers have suggested that New Zealand's musical history is distinctive not only because of its mixture of Maori and South Pacific sounds with English, European and North American music, but also because of New Zealand's place at the "bottom of the world", as Split Enz would later sing. The rest of the world paid little attention to what New Zealand musicians were doing, and when it did, there were no expectations that any of them would accomplish much. Being from that small country had some benefits, but it could also be a significant barrier to getting noticed or being taken seriously elsewhere.

Finn moved away from Te Awamutu to complete his high school education at a boarding school in Auckland, where he and his friend Mike Chunn "took over the music room" with their "not very good" band. After graduation, having a strong interest in literature and writing, Finn enrolled in a Bachelor of Arts degree program at the University of Auckland. Phil Judd had been a standout art student at Hastings Boys' High School, which led to him winning a place at the University's Elam Fine Arts School. In '71, their first year at the University, Finn and Judd became part of a group of students that hung out in and around room 129 in O'Rorke Hall, one of the University's student residences. Chunn described O'Rorke as "a place of madness [where] water bombs rained down on visitors and rockets flew down the corridors". Along with musical jamming, the habitues of 129 shared with each other their various artistic influences, "from Rembrandt to Yellow Dog comix, Dali to Robert Crumb to the MC5", and also, as one did at the time, experimented with drugs and other consciousness-altering substances.

While Finn and Judd enjoyed some of their classes, they disliked the bureaucracy and hierarchies of academia; Judd found art school to be "lectures and more lectures, and I just wanted to paint." By '72, both had dropped out of university and had started to form the earliest version of Split Ends. '129' was one of Judd and Finn's earliest collaborations, written during the year after they left university and concentrated on making music. The song portrays some of the creative experiences of the 129 crowd - terrified performers teetering on the edge of stage fright; the glamour of live shows undercut by uninterested audiences and seedy venues; jaunty rhythms juxtaposed with blissful, spiraling string crescendos. In retrospect, one observer wrote, "they had the scope and they began to use it, interweaving music hall, symphony, hard rock and dance band to create their present bedazzling, forever surprising, sound."

Split Ends' first major live appearance was at '73's Great Ngaruawahia Music Festival, New Zealand's first multi-day outdoor music event, staged in a rural setting on the North Island. As a mostly acoustic quartet, playing the mainstage in a prime evening time slot, Split Ends were booed so loudly and thoroughly that the event promoter told them to get off the stage. But '129' made its live debut as the final song in the band's unexpectedly abbreviated set. Split Ends gradually became better known and were better received as the band members improved their performance skills, but much to the frustration of their manager, Barry Coburn, they flatly refused to play the pub circuit that was the traditional breeding ground for fledgling New Zealand bands. Searching for other ways to promote his young clients, Coburn decided to enter Split Ends in *New Faces*, a nationally televised talent competition.

In May '73 the band entered a studio to pre-record '129', and on November 18 they travelled down to Wellington to perform on the *New Faces* broadcast. At home in Te Awamutu, Tim's father Richard used his 8-millimeter movie camera to film the television screen in the Finns' living room while Split Ends were performing. The restored footage, posted by Judd on YouTube, shows a fresh-faced group of long-haired young men that, even at this early stage, have what Finn biographer Jeff Apter characterizes as "a sense of self-assurance...while viewing their art as a very serious business, not some commercial commodity." Split Ends placed well enough in the first round of *New Faces* to win a spot in the final, but they had to play a different song for the last stage of the competition. They chose the slightly odder 'Sweet Talkin' Spoon Song' which the judges deemed "too clever" and "too complex". Split Ends finished seventh out of eight acts in the *New Faces* final, but the television appearances helped the band gain its first recording contract. Their first single was the winsome 'For You', produced by Coburn; '129' ended up as the B-side of their second single, 'Sweet Talkin' Spoon Song' (which Judd later said was his favourite Split Enz song ever).

Neither single was a commercial success, and Judd, deciding that he was no longer interested in playing live, departed the band. The rest of Split Enz soldiered on, heartened by more recording opportunities and increasingly larger audiences. Judd eventually decided to rejoin, although by this point he and Finn were largely writing and composing independently of each other. The addition of Noel Crombie – the visionary who was largely responsible for the band's colourful matching outfits, highly stylized hair, and exaggeratedly theatrical makeup – further tightened Split Enz into a going concern.

The group moved to Australia in '75, but struggled to connect with audiences more interested in hearing bell-bottomed boogie rock and roll. However, a gig opening for Roxy Music in Melbourne introduced the band to Roxy guitarist Phil Manzanera. Manzanera expressed an interest in producing the band's first album, but he was not available when Split Enz was scheduled to enter the studio in Australia. So the band ended up co-producing *Mental Notes* themselves, with Judd supplying the painting that became the cover art. The success of that album in Australia and New Zealand, along with the support of new management, brought Split Enz to the UK in '76 to record with Manzanera.

The band arrived in London just as the punk movement was beginning to make itself known. The band's theatrical costuming and makeup was simultaneously wildly out of touch with punk and also highly sympathetic to it as a visual expression of rebellion. At the end of one Split Enz gig, Finn recalls, a group of punks in full safety-pins-and-rags regalia stood in front of the stage, loudly debating whether it was okay or not to like the band. When Split Enz went into the studio, according to Chunn, Manzanera decided that the second album would be a mixture of re-recorded tracks from *Mental Notes* and a selection of the band's older songs, including '129'. Judd claims that while the members of Split Enz liked Manzanera and were grateful for his help, they "were pretty much told" by their record company and management to follow whatever Manzarena chose to do. Judd felt that "a great opportunity was lost" by the group not being able to include more new music.

'129' was not only rearranged but was also re-titled as 'Matinee Idyll', a bit of clever wordplay taken from its lyrics. The original '129' started with the noises of clinking glasses and pub chatter, gradually fading into a ukulele strum. The rearrangement of the new 'Matinee Idyll' kicked off with a lively piano-and-strings rhythm, and Finn's vocals were noticeably stronger and less mannered. The band also brought in former member Miles Golding, who played violin on '129' and was in London studying classical violin, to contribute to the updated track. Many of the differences between the arrangements of '129' and 'Matinee Idyll' are subtle, such as

Judd's vocal interjections being much further down in the mix of the latter, but 'Matinee Idyll' is tighter and more assertive, without losing the sense of the band's distinctive character.

The Manzanera-produced *Second Thoughts* charted in Australia and the UK, and the *New Musical Express* declared it "debut of the year". But despite critical praise, it did not sell in significant amounts. Split Enz fans have long debated the strategic wisdom of releasing a second album that partially included songs from the first album, thus putting two different versions of some songs on the market. The potential for confusion was further exacerbated when *Second Thoughts* was released in some regions under the title *Mental Notes*. 'Matinee Idyll' was one of two singles from *Second Thoughts*, but it and the other single, 'Late Last Night', failed to chart. Judd has said that making *Second Thoughts* was "a big step forward" for the band but the end product "didn't seem appropriate for the times".

Split Enz subsequently had major international successes – the hit singles 'I See Red', 'I Got You' and 'Six Months in a Leaky Boat' – and came tantalizingly close to top-tier success several times. But it seemed that twists of fate, such as changes in management and personnel, regularly derailed its career. Judd left the band permanently in the middle of a '77 US tour, and went on to his own successes with The Swingers and 'Counting the Beat'. Judd's replacement, Neil Finn, was in the band through its greatest popularity, and kept it going after his brother Tim wavered between it and a solo career. The strongest album from the post-Judd period may also be the band's greatest achievement: '81's *Time and Tide*, a musical journey that navigates a wondrously big world and the process of finding one's place in it.

Split Enz officially called it a day in late '84, but '129'/'Matinee Idyll' is regularly included in its greatest-hits and best-of compilations. It's also been on the set list of most of the band's reunion and anniversary concerts - the most recent, in 2006, can be heard on the 2017 CD *Alive Alive Oh*. '129'/'Matinee Idyll' continues to epitomize the bold creativity that gave a group from a small country the confidence and vision to do big things.

The True Wheel
Eno
1974

Art rock. The very words can induce repulsion even in experienced music fans. The phrase evokes shadowy stages populated by intensely grim-faced figures clad in black, hunched over odd-looking instruments that produce random atonal squonks intended to convey the meaninglessness of human existence and industrial civilization. Or something. Suffice it to say that art rock generally has the image of being very serious, very high-minded, and very weird.

Since Brian Eno is both a serious artist and a musician, his records tend to get mindlessly labeled as "art rock", or, more recently, as "ambient music". But those categorizations overlook the fact that in the early '70s, he produced a series of albums that are terrifically accessible and enjoyable. 'The True Wheel' from '74's *Taking Tiger Mountain By Strategy* is one of the lesser-covered songs from this era of Eno's work, but it has an interesting origin. And with its exuberant guitars, hammering piano, and girly vocals, followed by a jittery, staccato extended coda, it's also a great deal of fun.

In addition to being a musician, Eno is also the producer of such hugely successful albums as U2's *The Joshua Tree* and Coldplay's *Viva La Vida*, but his first notable musical venture was as a member of Roxy Music. He was trained as a visual artist, and during his art school days he became interested in electronic and avant-garde music, particularly the manipulation of recorded sounds on tape. He was also a clarinet player in the Scratch Orchestra and then the Portsmouth Sinfonia, both of which were musical ensembles that required no instrumental competence to join; anyone who has endured the noises made by a beginning clarinet player will appreciate that it likely takes a special type of brave to inflict that racket on an audience.

Thankfully, in '70 when Eno encountered his old friend Andy Mackay on the Tube in London, Mackay was more interested in Eno's tape machines than in his clarinet skills. Mackay recruited Eno to help him record a demo for the band he had just joined. Mackay also owned a VCS3 "Putney", one of the first portable synthesizers, but hadn't had much time to learn how it worked. He lent it to Eno, and the skills that Eno developed with this new technology, along with his recording expertise and interest in experimental music, led to him joining Roxy Music as "sound manipulator". Roxy Music's rise to fame has been chronicled in great detail elsewhere, but most sources concur that as the band's popularity grew, conflicts arose between Eno and vocalist/frontman Bryan Ferry. Ferry felt that Eno was unjustifiably receiving more attention and praise than he did. Eno felt that the band's music was increasingly following Ferry's vision rather than using all of its members' ideas and talents.

A frustrated Eno departed Roxy Music in '73. His first post-Roxy album, released that same year, was *(No Pussyfooting)*, a collaboration with guitarist Robert Fripp. The album explored innovative uses of studio techniques, particularly looping, in which a sound was created and replayed with additional aural effects being layered over each repetition. Eno's first individual album was '74's *Here Come the Warm Jets* – the title, according to Eno biographer David Sheppard, coming from Eno's description of the "treated guitar sound" on the record as the sound of approaching jets. The album's tracks drew on recognizable pop song formats, but stretched those formats with unusual sound effects and stream-of-consciousness lyrics. Perhaps surprisingly for listeners who might have known Eno only as Roxy's glam-and-feathers synthesizer whiz, *Warm Jets* also showed him to be a competent vocalist, with an archly knowing tone to his voice.

Taking Tiger Mountain, released later in '74, came across as a more unified effort than *Warm Jets*. According to Sheppard, *Tiger Mountain*'s creation was more structured that the previous album's; Eno enlisted his ex-Roxy colleague Phil Manzanera to sort through Eno's "swollen tape library and assorted Dictaphone doodles" and to winnow out whatever could be used as the starting points for songs. Another difference was that the album was shaped by a "coherent conceptual approach" inspired by a set of postcards Eno had purchased in San Francisco's Chinatown, depicting scenes from a "propagandist Maoist" Chinese ballet that told the story of a battle between the Liberation Army and the imperialist forces. Eno's interest in "strategy" drew him to the ballet's title, and this interest was also apparent in how he approached putting together his new songs. He drew flow charts outlining each one's structure, including places where the lyrics would "sit", and then would populate those places either with phrases or words that caught his fancy, or with lyrics that he spontaneously sang in the studio. This method of working, including Eno's ongoing stream of notes to himself, eventually developed into the Oblique Strategies card deck – a set of individual and unconnected statements, intended to inspire creativity - which Eno created with his artist friend Peter Schmidt.

Eno also tried to upend how pop songs were usually put together. He wanted to "alter the angle of the song" by putting the background singers at the front. He also "wanted to make something that was like the voice of a group of people who had done something together, or were about to do something together". 'The True Wheel' provided an ideal opportunity to explore that approach, as it was based on a dream that starred a group chorale. "In New York I went to stay with this girl called Randi and fell asleep after taking some mescaline and had this dream where this group of girls were singing to this group of sailors who had just come into port. And they were singing 'We are the 801/We are the Central Shaft' – and I woke up absolutely jubilant because this was the first bit of lyric I'd written in this new style."

As with most things discussed on the Internet, there are numerous explanations of the "real" meaning of the lyrics of 'The True Wheel'. '801' has been identified as an acronym for Eno's surname (Eight Nought One); as the numerical representation of God in certain numeric-alphabetic systems; and a reference to the eight ethnicities identified in some theories of racial superiority – which, some argue, is supported by the chant of "looking for a certain ratio" in 'The True Wheel''s call-and-response middle section. The female chorus on the song is credited to "Randi and the Pyramids", although opinions vary as to whether Eno's New York friend 'Randi' is actually one of the singers. Manzanera later recalled that he contributed "the chord structure" to the song, for which he received one of the few co-writing credits on the album.

Taking Tiger Mountain By Strategy was not as well received than *Here Come The Warm Jets* and the two later Eno albums (*Another Green World* and *Before and After Science*), but the '801' moniker later reappeared as the name of the performing band assembled in '76 by Eno and Manzanera. 801 played three live concerts, excerpts from which were assembled into the album *801 Live*, and made one studio album, *Listen Now*. While 801's repertoire included several songs from Eno's solo albums, 'The True Wheel' didn't make the cut. That means, as far as I can tell, that Eno himself has never played 'The True Wheel' live – which is really a loss for such a dynamic and catchy song.

When Eno's four '70s albums were recently remastered and re-released, it was Manzanera that participated in the publicity campaign. Given that, there didn't seem to be much point in trying to track down Eno for a chat about 'The True Wheel'. But, thanks to the wonderland that is YouTube, I came across Music for Enophiles, a New York-based ensemble which plays concerts featuring numbers from those four early-'70s Eno albums, and which does a fantastic version of 'The True Wheel'. So I talked to Larry Heinemann, Music for Enophiles' founder and leader, about his experiences with the song.

Heinemann grew up in the eastern US and first encountered *Taking Tiger Mountain By Strategy* on his 13th birthday, when an older sibling gave him the album as a present. "It just sort of became this landmark record for me. It was so weird, the music was so weird, but from the moment I dropped the needle on 'Burning Airlines Give You So Much More', a light went off and I just really liked it. And it was sort of a secret, because no one else I knew had this record. And the artwork, I would endlessly look at the sleeve and the little treated photographs of Eno – just everything about it was somehow unlikely but it caught my fancy." Throughout his career as a professional musician, composer, and producer, he always had the idea of some kind of Eno act in the back of his mind, but he didn't want to do a "tribute"-type show that reproduced the music exactly. "That never feels very rock and roll to me. It feels somewhere in between rock and roll and musical theatre, and I really didn't want to do that. I was just picturing, what would be my best case scenario in a band playing Eno stuff? And it would just be a really good band that would play the crap out of the songs."

To realize his vision, he recruited six other musicians, most of whom he had previously worked with on other projects, but not all of whom were familiar with the '70s Eno records. "I'd say that half of them were pretty steeped, and the other half were - I'd say, check this out, this is something you want to do. And then everyone was on board." When choosing the songs, he went for "what I would be excited by seeing live and what would be tenable. And what would be kind of natural for us to play, that we aren't just killing ourselves trying to play, but can play it organically as if we wrote it, as a song of ours." 'The True Wheel' made the cut because "it's a monster, live. The first time we played it live, in front of people, the guitar solo is brutal. It's intense on the record, but it turns into like the hard rock Freebird solo. One of the lifetime performing highlights for me was seeing the life that the tune took on, and the audience, it just blew their heads off, in a way that – I mean it sounded good in rehearsal. But that's a natural song, it's just got such a cool evolution the way it devolves with the outro and the vocals, and having a drummer and a percussionist on it – it's such a natural performance song." 'The True Wheel' is also particularly suited for Music for Enophiles because the band has four vocalists, "so the verse can be broken up into the call-and-response, which is nice theatrically. It's a lot of fun to sing."

Heinemann has sent a letter to Eno's management to let him know about Music for Enophiles; "I haven't heard anything back, but I have a fantasy that one day we'd get to play this stuff in front of him." Meanwhile, Music for Enophiles, in Heinemann's words, "is like a public service in playing these songs for Eno fans, which we're more than happy to oblige. People really seem to dig it. I've had a couple of people say they almost like hearing it live better, or it gave them a new appreciation for hearing the songs live with a band."

Eno has a decades-long reputation as a restless creative soul who generally refuses to revisit his artistic past. But in 2003, San Francisco musicians Doug Hilsinger and Caroleen Beatty, who also play live as EnOrchestra, created a record that was a track-by-track cover of the entire *Tiger Mountain* album. As it happened, not long after the record was completed, Eno was giving a lecture in San Francisco, and Hilsinger was able to give Eno a CD with the rough mix of the project. Much to Hilsinger's astonishment, Eno phoned him a few days later to express his admiration for their work. In a later email, Eno wrote, "When I did these songs, they were very much experiments to me – I can honestly say that I wasn't thinking of them as music. I don't know what they were. When I heard your versions, I thought, 'Gosh, they were music after all!'". So maybe when Eno does look back at his work, he has come to realize that 'The True Wheel' might have started out as 'art rock', but grew into a song loved by both record buyers and live audiences – and, by now, to listeners who might not even have been born when it was made. That kind of longevity is the mark of great art *and* of great music.

BIBLIOGRAPHY

General Sources

Discogs www.discogs.com
Rock's Backpages www.rocksbackpages.com
SecondHand Songs www.secondhandsongs.com
Setlist.fm: The Setlist Wiki www.setlist.fm
YouTube www.youtube.com

Chapter Sources

When You Walk in the Room
A Boat Against the Current [blog] (2014). Song lyric of the day: Jackie DeShannon on the magic 'When You Walk in the Room'. 21 August. http://boatagainstthecurrent.blogspot.com/2014/08/song-lyric-of-day-jackie-deshannon-on.html
Barnes, K. (1974). *Various artists: Mersey Beat '62-'64* [review]. *Phonograph Record*, December issue.
Cerf, M. (1975). Jackie DeShannon: Creemcheese. *Phonograph Record*, October issue.
Conqueroo (2011). Jackie DeShannon's 'When You Walk in the Room' revisits influential singer-songwriter's hits. *No Depression*, 11 July. http://nodepression.com/article/jackie-deshannons-when-you-walk-room-revisits-influential-singer-songwriters-hits
Gross, T. (2010). What the world needs now is Jackie DeShannon. Interview for National Public Radio (NPR) program *Fresh Air*, 10 June. https://www.npr.org/templates/story/story.php?storyId=127541549
Helander, B. (1999). *The rockin' '60s: The people who made the music*. New York: Schirmer Trade Books.

Jones, P. (1964). Jackie DeShannon: Jackie jumps for joy. *Record Mirror*, 7 November.

Kubernik, H. (2000). Legendary music arranger and composer, Jack Nitzsche, dies. *Rock's Backpages*, September.

Morrison, C. (2008). The Searchers: Interview with bassist Frank Allen. http://www.craigmorrison.com/spip.php?article81

Rogers, J. (2009). Jackie DeShannon: Return of the starry-eyed girl. *The Guardian*, 1 May.

Tootell, R. (2008). Got live if you want it?: Bruce Springsteen on stage, 1968-2005. *Rock's Backpages*, July.

Tyler, K. (2001). Jimmy Page: Educating Jimmy. *MOJO*, May issue.

Iko Iko

Abbey, J. (1979). The Neville Brothers: A family affair. *Blues and Soul*, February issue.

Dr. John's Gumbo (1972). Liner notes from original release, SD 7006.

Grateful Dead Family Discography (n.d.) Iko Iko. http://www.deaddisc.com/songs/Iko_Iko.htm

Griffiths, D. (1966). The Dixie Cups: Dixie's dream city is Manchester. *Record Mirror*, 10 December.

Hannusch, J. (2002). James 'Sugar Boy' Crawford. *Offbeat*, 2 February. http://www.offbeat.com/articles/james-sugar-boy-crawford/

Hinshaw, D. (2009). Iko Iko: in search of Jockomo. *Offbeat*, 1 April. http://www.offbeat.com/articles/iko-iko-in-search-of-jockomo/

Marshall, M. (2012). Mardi Gras! A brief history of "Iko! Iko! Jock-a-mo Fee No Nay". *American Blues Scene*, 17 February. https://www.americanbluesscene.com/iko-iko-jock-a-mo/

Rosenthal, E. (2001). *His song: The musical journey of Elton John*. New York: Billboard Books.

Staunton, T. (1998). Film pop-stars: *This* much talent! *Uncut*, December issue.

White, C. (1976). The Wild Tchoupitoulas: *The Wild Tchoupitoulas* (Island)/ The Meters: *The Best Of...* [album review]. *New Musical Express*, 24 July.

Williams, R. (2009). Ellie Greenwich, 1940-2009. The Guardian, 27 August https://www.theguardian.com/music/2009/aug/27/ellie-greenwich-obituary

Morning of My Life/In the Morning
Aizlewood, J. (1994). *Love is the drug: Living as a pop fan*. London: Penguin Books.

Black, J. (2001). The Bee Gees: The rogue gene. *MOJO*, June issue.

Brennan, J. (2015). Gibb Songs [website]. http://www.columbia.edu/~brennan/beegees/

Deevoy, A. (1989). The Bee Gees: Forgive and forget. *Q*, June issue.

Hughes, A.M. (2009). *The Bee Gees: Tales of the Brothers Gibb*. London: Omnibus Press.

Milesago [n.d.]. Ronnie Burns. Milesago Australasian Music and Popular Culture 1964-1975 [blog]. http://www.milesago.com/Artists/burns.htm

Richmond, P. [n.d.] Mary Hopkin timeline, 1968. Mary Hopkin Friendly Society. http://www.maryhopkin.com/pages/mhfs-timeline.html

Sunny Goodge Street
Brisebois, D. (2017). Tom Northcott discography. http://www.canadianbands.com/Tom%20Northcott.html

Dallas, K. (1966). Collins: A singer, period. *Melody Maker*, 12 November.

Draai weer bij [n.d.] http://www.boudewijndegroot.nl/component/discografie/?view=liedteksten&id=10

Leitch, D. (2005). *The autobiography of Donovan: The hurdy gurdy man*. New York: St. Martin's Press.

Saltzman, P. [n.d.] The Beatles in India: Donovan. https://thebeatlesinindia.com/stories/donovan/

Unterberger, R. (2005). Donovan. *MOJO*, January issue.

Vas, M. (2014). Donovan's music banned in South Africa. https://www.facebook.com/251922131233/photos/donovan%E2%80%99s-music-banned-in-south/10152238635926234/

Reason to Believe

Bardach, A.L. (1980). *The heavy heart of Tim Hardin.* Interview originally published in WET magazine, September. http://www.bardachreports.com/articles/int_19800900.html

Carpenter, R. (2004) *Song notes: 'Reason to Believe'.* https://www.richardandkarencarpenter.com/SN_ReasonToBelieve.htm

Gavin, J. (2015). *Is that all there is?: The strange life of Peggy Lee.* New York: Simon & Schuster.

Gillett, C. (1996). *The sound of the city: The rise of rock and roll (2nd ed.).* New York: Da Capo Press.

Johnson, J. (1972). Tim Hardin [audio interview]. https://www.rocksbackpages.com/Library/Article/tim-hardin-1972

Mathieson, B. (2013). Hanging on…to the dream [Tim Hardin website]. http://www.songsinger.info/th/biograph.html

Pidgeon, J. (2010). *I was a Faces roadie (Part 1).* November 22. http://www.johnpidgeon.com/words/?p=33

Ragogna, M. (2009). The 40th anniversary of Carpenters: Interview with Richard Carpenter. *Huffington Post*, 6. June. https://www.huffingtonpost.com/mike-ragogna/emhuffpost-exclusiveem-th_b_201408.html

Reason to believe: The real Tim Hardin (2005). BBC Radio 2 documentary. http://www.bbc.co.uk/radio2/r2music/documentaries/timhardin.shtml

Santiago-Mercado, M. (n.d.) *Peggy Lee's bio-discography: The Capitol years, part VII (1968-1972).* http://www.peggyleediscography.com/p/capitolee2c.php

Starr, M. (2004). *Bobby Darin: A life.* Guilford, CT: Taylor Trade Publishing.

Unterberger, R. (n.d.) Bobby Darin: *If I Were a Carpenter*. https://www.allmusic.com/album/if-i-were-a-carpenter-mw0000849193

A Place in the Sun
Author interview with Bryan Wells, November 2017.
Dalton, D., & Kaye, L. (1976). *Rock 100: The all-stars from rock & roll's hall of fame*. New York: Putnam.
Gordy, B. (1994). *To be loved: The music, the magic, the memories of Motown*. New York: Time Warner Publishing.
Hoskyns, B. (2005). Stevie Wonder takes his *Time*. *Uncut*, June issue.
Lodder, S. (2005). *Stevie Wonder: A musical guide to the classic albums*. San Francisco: Backbeat Books.
Nixon, T. (2012). Marvin Gaye: 'My Way'. *Motown Junkies* [blog], 8 August. https://motownjunkies.co.uk/2012/08/21/520/
OWN [Oprah Winfrey Network] (2013). Berry Gordy on Motown: 'I was in charge, but I made logic the boss'. *Huffington Post*, 18 June. https://www.huffingtonpost.com/2013/06/18/berry-gordy-motown-meetings_n_3455197.html
Posner, G. (2002). *Motown: Money, music, sex and power*. New York: Random House.
Ribowsky, M. (2010). *Ain't too proud to beg: The troubled lives and enduring soul of the Temptations*. Hoboken, NJ: Wiley.
Ribowsky, M. (2010). *Signed, sealed, delivered: The soulful journey of Stevie Wonder*. Hoboken, NJ: Wiley.
Turner, T., & Aria, B. (1990). *All that glittered: My life with the Supremes*. New York: Dutton.
Turner, T. & Aria, B. (2002). *Deliver us from temptation: The tragic and shocking story of the Temptations and Motown*. New York: Thunder's Mouth Press.
Werner, C. (1999). Stevie Wonder: Singing in the key of life. *Goldmine*, October 8.
Williams, O., & Romanowski, P. (2002). *Temptations*. New York: Cooper Square Press.

Wasn't It You

Barnard, J. (2017). Walking in angels' footsteps. *Shindig!*, August issue.

Bernstein, A, (2014). Gerry Goffin, lyricist who co-wrote seminal '60s hits, dies at 75. *The Washington Post*, 20 June. https://www.washingtonpost.com/entertainment/music/gerry-goffin-lyricist-who-co-wrote-seminal-60s-hits-dies-at-75/2014/06/20/424c2c1e-f7fe-11e3-8aa9-dad2ec039789_story.html?utm_term=.30bf2fa32818

Brown, H. (2016). Carole King interview: 'I didn't have the courage to write songs initially'. *The Telegraph*, 7 March. https://www.telegraph.co.uk/music/artists/carole-king-interview-i-didnt-have-the-courage-to-write-songs-in/

Cohen, M. (1976). Carole King: On this side of goodbye. *Phonograph Record*, January issue.

Freeman, V. (2008). Brent Titcomb: 3's a Crowd. 28 August. https://web.archive.org/web/20080828021607/http://www.brenttitcomb.com/crowd.html

Frith, S. (1973). Billie Davis: Woman in pop. *Let It Rock*, September issue.

Gross, T. (2013). For Carole King, songwriting is a 'natural' talent. Interview for National Public Radio (NPR) program *Fresh Air*, 23 June. https://www.npr.org/2013/06/28/196326148/for-carole-king-songwriting-is-a-natural-talent

Hibbert, T. (1982). *Rare records: Wax trash and vinyl treasures*. London: Proteus Publishing.

'John Mayall, Love, Petula Clark et al: Albums' (1966). *Melody Maker*, 6 August.

Jones, N. (1966). The Action: Shoreline Club, Bognor Regis. *Melody Maker*, 3 September.

King, C. (2012). *A natural woman: A memoir*. New York: Grand Central Publishing.

Weller, S. (2009). *Girls like us: Carole King, Joni Mitchell, Carly Simon – and the journey of a generation*. New York: Atria Books.

The First Cut is the Deepest

American Society of Composers, Authors and Performers [ASCAP] (2006). *Yusuf Islam named Songwriter of the Year at ASCAP Awards in London.* 11 October. https://www.ascap.com/press/2006/101106_prs.html

Bangs, L. (1977). Rod Stewart: *The Best of Rod Stewart, Vol. 2*; The Faces: *Snakes and Ladders – The Best of the Faces* [album review]. *Circus*, 28 April.

De Bertodano, H. (2014). Sheryl Crow interview: 'I've quit letting people run over me'. *The Telegraph*, 26 October. https://www.telegraph.co.uk/culture/music/rockandpopfeatures/11177789/Sheryl-Crow-interview-Ive-quit-letting-people-run-over-me.html

Gregor, K. (2017). [producer]. *Soul Music: 'First Cut is the Deepest'*. Series 20, Episode 3. BBC Radio 4, 20 October. https://www.bbc.co.uk/programmes/b05s2x2k

Irwin, C. (2000). Cat Stevens: Time to make a change. *MOJO*, June issue.

Jones, P. (1967). Who, Prince Buster, Bee Gees et al: New singles reviewed. *Record Mirror*, 22 April.

Mason, P. (2018). Oldies still goodies: PP Arnold and Mavis Staples deliver blistering sets at the Cornbury Festival. *Morning Star*, 17 July. https://morningstaronline.co.uk/article/oldies-still-goldies

Rock and Roll Hall of Fame [n.d.] Cat Stevens. https://www.rockhall.com/inductees/cat-stevens

Scoppa, B. (1976). Rod Stewart: *A Night On The Town*. *Phonograph Record*, August issue.

Stewart, R. (2012). *Rod: The autobiography*. London: Century.

Tobler, J., & Grundy, S., (1983). Tom Dowd. *The record producers*. London: St. Martin's Press.

Wale, M. (1972). *Voxpop: Profiles of the pop process*. London: Harrap.

The Worst That Could Happen

DeMain, B. (2001). *Behind the muse: Pop and rock's greatest songwriters talk about their work and inspiration.* Cranberry Township, PA: Tiny Ripple Books.

DeYoung, B. (1999). Up up and away: Jimmy Webb and The 5th Dimension. *Goldmine*, 10 September.

Dolan, J. (2017). Jimmy Webb on John Lennon's lost weekend, writing for Frank Sinatra. *Rolling Stone*, 18 April. https://www.rollingstone.com/music/music-features/jimmy-webb-on-john-lennons-lost-weekend-writing-for-frank-sinatra-118453/

Everett, T. (1977). Jimmy Webb: Ten years after 'Phoenix' he's still looking for Hit City. *Phonograph Record*, June issue.

Hoskyns, B. (1997). Jimmy Webb: *Ten Easy Pieces. MOJO*, September issue.

Hoskyns, B. (2005). Almost blue: Jimmy Webb. *Uncut*, June issue.

I Hear Voices! [2016] Suzy Ronstadt biography. http://www.ihearvoicessinging.com/SuzyPage.html

Irvin, J. (1997). Jimmy Webb: an interview [unpublished]. http://www.rocksbackpages.com/Library/Article/jimmy-webb-an-interview

Lewis, R. (2013). Muse for Jimmy Webb's 'MacArthur Park' treasures those days. *Los Angeles Times*, 20 July. http://articles.latimes.com/2013/jul/20/entertainment/la-et-ms-suzy-ronstadt-20130720

Morten, A. (2008). The 5th Dimension: *The Magic Garden* [liner notes for re-release]. Rev-Ola Records.

Rosen, C. (2013). Nilsson & Jimmy Webb: Let me tell you about my best friend. *Rolling Stone*, 25 July. https://www.rollingstone.com/music/music-news/nilsson-jimmy-webb-let-me-tell-you-about-my-best-friend-91985/

Sculatti, G. (2006). The 5th Dimension: *Up, Up and Away/The Magic Garden* [liner notes for re-release]. Collector's Choice Records.

Webb, J. (1998). *Tunesmith: Inside the art of songwriting.* New York: Hyperion.

Webb. J. (2017). *The cake and the rain: A memoir.* New York: St. Martin's Press.

Living Without You

Bryant, D. (2010). Keith Shields – *'Deep Inside Your Mind'/'Hey Gyp (Dig the Slowness)'*. Left and to the Back [blog], 28 April. http://left-and-to-the-back.blogspot.com/2010/04/keith-shields-deep-inside-your-mind-hey.html

Courrier, K. (2005). *Randy Newman's American dreams.* Toronto: ECW Press.

Denisoff, R. Serge. (1975). *Solid gold: The popular record industry*. Piscataway, NJ: Transaction Publishers.

Dylan, J. (2016). My favorite album: Van Dyke Parks on Randy Newman's *'Randy Newman'* [podcast]. 12 June. http://mrjeremydylan.com/post/145828409205/my-favorite-album-141-van-dyke-parks-on-randy

Felton, D. (1972). Randy Newman: You've got to let this fat boy in your life. *Rolling Stone*, 31 August. https://www.rollingstone.com/music/music-news/randy-newman-youve-got-to-let-this-fat-boy-in-your-life-106154/

Friedersdorf, D. (2017). The *dark matter* of America's foremost musical satirist. *The Atlantic*, 16 August. https://www.theatlantic.com/entertainment/archive/2017/08/the-dark-matter-of-americas-foremost-musical-satirist/536262/

Hoskyns, B. (1998). Randy Newman: 'I love you, you c**t!' *MOJO*, August issue.

MacDonald, I. (1998). Randy Newman: Here comes the rain. *Uncut*, August issue.

Partridge, R. (1974). Randy Newman: 'I'd like to have a hit'. *Melody Maker*. 15 June.

Phipps, K. (2003). Interview: Randy Newman. *AV Club*, 10 August. https://www.avclub.com/randy-newman-1798208294

Saunders, M. (1972). Manfred Mann: *Manfred Mann's Earth Band* (album review). *Rolling Stone*, 30 March.

Technicolor Web of Sound [n.d.] Artist profile: Keith Shields. http://www.techwebsound.com/playlistdetail.cfm?previous=780

Waronker, L. (1998). The man, the music. *Guilty: 30 years of Randy Newman* [liner notes for box set]. Rhino/Warner Archives Records.

White, T. (1998). Bet no one ever hurt this bad: The importance of being Randy Newman. *Guilty: 30 years of Randy Newman* [liner notes for box set]. Rhino/Warner Archives Records.

I'm the Urban Spaceman

Alterman, L. (1969). Bonzo Dog runs, fucks itself. *Rolling Stone*, 29 November.

Carruthers, B., & Christie, D. (2011). *The Bonzo Dog Doo-Dah Band: Jollity Farm*. London: Coda Books.

Kaplan, I. (2014). Neil Innes [Yo La Tengo website]. 7 October. http://yolatengo.com/neil-innes/

Mungo Jerry 1971-72. Mungo Jerry Magic [website]. http://www.mungojerrymagic.com/1971-2/

Randall, L., & Welch, C. (2001). *Ginger geezer: The life of Vivian Stanshall*. London: Fourth Estate Publishers.

Rogan, J. (1988). *Starmakers and Svengalis: The history of British pop management*. London: Trans-Atlantic Publishers.

Sounes, H. (2010). *Fab: An intimate life of Paul McCartney*. New York: Doubleday.

Feelin' Alright

Altham, K. (1972). The Joe Cocker ritual sacrifice. *New Musical Express*, 20 May.

Briggs, C. (1974). *Dave Mason*. ZigZag, March issue.

Cott, J. (1969). Traffic: the Rolling Stone interview. *Rolling Stone*, 9 May. https://www.rollingstone.com/music/features/traffic-interview-19690503

DeYoung, B. (1996). We just disagree: The story of Dave Mason. *Goldmine*, 16 February.

Frame, P. (1983). *Rock Family Trees, Volume 2*. London: Omnibus Press.

Jahn, M. (1969). Joe Cocker & the Grease Band: Fillmore East, New York, NY. *The New York Times*, 10 August.

Rensin, D. (1974). Dave Mason: No more Traffic jams. *Rolling Stone*, 14 March.

Schaffner, N. (1983). *The British Invasion: From the First Wave to the New Wave*. New York: Straight Arrow/McGraw-Hill.

Scoppa, B. (1982). Joe Cocker: The A&M years 1968-1976. Unpublished.

"Traffic" [n.d.]. http://www.brumbeat.net/traffic.htm

"The Traffic Cottage at Aston-Tirrold" [n.d.]. http://www.winwoodfans.com/aston.htm

Valentine, P. (1972). Joe Cocker: 'With A Song in Your Heart'. *Sounds*, 18 November.

Think of Rain

Anders, T. (2015). Margo Guryan: Dream, plan, hope, imagine. *LA Record*, 20 November. http://larecord.com/archive/2015/11/20/margo-guryan-interview

Author interview with Margo Guryan, November 2016.

Breznikar, K. (2018). Margo Guryan interview. *It's Psychedelic Baby* [online magazine]. http://www.psychedelicbabymag.com/2018/03/margo-guryan-interview.html

Frank, P. (2018). One-album wonder Margo Guryan didn't fade away. She escaped. *Huffington Post*, 7 March. https://www.huffingtonpost.ca/entry/margo-guryan-music-industry_us_5aa16fd0e4b0e9381c16951b

Glauber, G. (2001). Margo Guryan: 25 Demos. *Pop Matters*, 3 September. https://www.popmatters.com/guryanmargo-25demos-2495923517.html

Juhan, J. (2016). Interview with Margo Guryan. *The Weekly Tryst*, WCSF radio, 16 January. https://soundcloud.com/wcsf-1/margo-guryan-interview

Record World (1968). Review of 'Spanky & Our Gang'/'Sunday Mornin''. 6 April. https://www.americanradiohistory.com/Archive-Record-World/60s/68/RW-1968-04-06.pdf

Abergavenny

Black, J. (1981). Kim Wilde: Wilde life. *Smash Hits*, 28 May.

Chapman, R. (2015). *Psychedelia and other colours*. London: Faber and Faber.

Savage, J. (1995). The Blackheath jungle. *MOJO*, February issue.

Savage, J. (1995). The great pretender. *MOJO*, February issue.

Simmons, S. (1986). The Moody Blues are older than you. *Creem*, December issue.

Stuart, J. (2001). Michael Biggs: The end of the line for a dutiful son? *The Independent*, 3 December. https://www.independent.co.uk/news/people/profiles/michael-biggs-the-end-of-the-line-for-a-dutiful-son-9252819.html

Thompson, D. (2010). *Children of the revolution: The glam rock story, 1970-75*. Chiswick, UK: Cherry Red Books.

Tobler, J., & Grundy, S., (1983). Mickie Most. *The record producers*. London: St. Martin's Press.

Turner, S. (1975). Larry Parnes. *New Musical Express*, 2 August.

Webber, R. (2014). Marty Wilde: 'I'd buy cars then sell them again a few days later'. *The Telegraph*, 24 February. https://www.telegraph.co.uk/finance/personalfinance/fameandfortune/10654752/Marty-Wilde-Id-buy-cars-then-sell-them-a-few-days-later.html

Neanderthal Man

Barber, S., & O'Connor, B. (2016). Sodajerker on songwriting: episode 95, Kevin Godley [podcast]. https://www.sodajerker.com/episode-95-kevin-godley/

Betrock, A. (1975). 10cc: The worst band in the world? *ZigZag*, January issue.

Bootleg Zone [blog] (n.d.) Elton John – *Reg Dwight's Piano Goes Pop*. http://www.bootlegzone.com/album.php?name=pianogoespop

Cooper, K., & Smay, D. (2001). *Bubblegum music is the naked truth: The dark history of prepubescent pop, from the Banana Splits to Britney Spears*. Los Angeles: Feral House.

Copycat Cover Records: Adventures in collecting anonymous cover versions [blog] (2012). *'Pick of the Pick of the Pops'*. 8 November. http://copycatcovers.blogspot.com/2012/11/pick-of-pick-of-pops.html

Ingham, J. (1975). 10cc and ready to roar. *Hit Parader*, November issue.

Norman, P. (1991). *Elton: The definitive biography*. London: Arrow Books.

Robinson, C. (2017). Stockport's Strawberry Recording Studios. *Playing Pasts*, 27 July. http://www.playingpasts.co.uk/articles/general/stockports-strawberry-recording-studios/

'Strawberry Studios: I Am In Love'. Exhibition at Stockport Museum, 27 January 2017 to 30 September 2018. https://www.strawberry50.com/exhibits/early-days/

Thompson, D. (2010). *Children of the revolution: The glam rock story, 1970-75*. Chiswick, UK: Cherry Red Books.

Lovin' You Ain't Easy

Billboard (1971). Canadian news report: CHUM refutes charge by CIRPA on airplay. 30 January, p. 55.

Brisebois, D. (n.d.) Michel Pagliaro. *Canadian Bands* [website]. http://www.canadianbands.com/home.html

Cashbox Canada (2013). Brian Chater: the best friend a song ever had. 19 September. http://cashboxcanada.ca/4360/brian-chater-best-friend-song-ever-had

CIMA [Canadian Independent Music Association] (2013). Remembering Brian Chater. 9 September.
https://cimamusic.ca/news/recent-news/read,article/1016/remembering-brian-chater

Gold, G.P. (2001). Ten Canadian records you can't live without. *Cosmik Debris*, April issue.

Governor General's Performing Arts Awards (2008). Michel Pagliaro: 2008 Lifetime Artistic Achievement (Popular Music). https://ggpaa.ca/award-recipients/2008/pagliaro-michel.aspx?lang=en-CA#!prettyPhoto

McCooey, P. (2017). Canadian rock legend Michel Pagliaro donates personal archives. *Ottawa Citizen*, 5 May. https://ottawacitizen.com/news/local-news/canadian-rock-legend-michel-pagliaro-donates-personal-archives

Pierson (2004). Greg Shaw's all-time power pop records, March 1978. Eric Carmen Forum [website]. http://ericcarmen.com/forums/index.php?/topic/16405-greg-shaws-all-time-power-pop-records-march-1978/

Provencher, R. (2017). Michel Pagliaro donates personal archives to Library and Archives Canada. 5 May. https://www.canada.ca/en/library-archives/news/2017/05/michel_pagliaro_donatespersonalarchivestolibraryandarchivescanad.html

Rioux, C. (2013). Michel Pagliaro. *The Canadian Encyclopedia*. https://www.thecanadianencyclopedia.ca/en/article/michel-pagliaro-emc

Shaw, G. (1973). Michel Pagliaro: *M'Lady/Pagliaro/Pag/Pagliaro Live* [album review]. *Phonograph Record*, March issue.

Zimbel, M. (2016). You can call me Pag: Québec's rebel superstar Michel Pagliaro. FYI Music News, 26 September. https://www.fyimusicnews.ca/articles/2016/09/26/you-can-call-me-pag-qu%C3%A9bec%E2%80%99s-rebel-superstar-michel-pagliaro

Everything Stops for Tea

Leviton, M. (1972). Long John Baldry meets Mad Mark Leviton. *UCLA Daily Bruin*, 10 August.

Murray, C.S. (1975). Elton John, part 2: They laughed when I stood up to play the piano. *New Musical Express*, 1 March.

Myers, P. (2007). *It ain't easy: Long John Baldry and the birth of the British blues*. Vancouver, BC: Greystone Books.

Salewicz, C. (1973). Long John Baldry: S'long John. *Let It Rock*, March issue.

Shaw, G. (1972). John Baldry: Everything Stops for Tea. *Rolling Stone*, 25 May.

Songfacts (n.d.) Everything Stops for Tea, by Jack Buchanan. http://www.songfacts.com/detail.php?id=21376

You Put Something Better Inside Me
ArtsWork Scotland (2012). *Gerry Rafferty: Right down the line*. BBC Two television documentary, 27 February. https://www.bbc.co.uk/programmes/b0140v4c

Black, J. (2011). *Gerry Rafferty: City to City* [album review]. *Hi-Fi News & Record Review*, March issue.

Daily Record (2011). Gerry Rafferty's daughter opens heart on how 'Baker Street' destroyed her dad. 14 August. https://www.dailyrecord.co.uk/entertainment/music/music-news/gerry-raffertys-daughter-opens-heart-1080694

Chandler, A. (2015). 'Baker Street': the mystery of rock's greatest sax riff. *The Atlantic*, 17 December. https://www.theatlantic.com/entertainment/archive/2015/12/baker-street-gerry-rafferty-saxophone/421008/

Gilbert, J. (1975). The Gerry Rafferty interview. *ZigZag*, August issue.

Laing, D. (1975). Stealers Wheel. *Let It Rock*, May issue.

Leiber, J., Stoller, M. & Ritz, D. (2009). *Hound dog: The Leiber & Stoller autobiography*. New York: Simon and Schuster.

Partridge, P. (1974). Stealers Wheel: Wheel of fortune. *Melody Maker*, 5 January.

Raphael Ravenscroft: Her Father Didn't Like Me Anyway [album review] (2009). Myreccollection [blog], 22 February. https://myreccollection.livejournal.com/297501.html

Rees, P. (2018). Remembering Gerry Rafferty, rock's most reluctant star. *Ultimate Classic Rock*, 4 January. https://www.loudersound.com/features/remembering-gerry-rafferty-rocks-most-reluctant-star

Sutcliffe, P. (2010). Gerry Rafferty. *MOJO*, February issue.

The man who was down to earth (1979). *Melody Maker*, 12 May. http://www.redstone-tech.com/gerry_bsb/melody_maker_1979.htm

Sail On Sailor
Bell, M. (1975). The Beach Boys and the Eagles at Wembley Stadium. *New Musical Express*, 28 June.

Brown, H. (2016). Bad vibrations: Where did it all go wrong for the Beach Boys? *The Telegraph*, 10 October. https://www.telegraph.co.uk/music/what-to-listen-to/bad-vibrations-where-did-it-all-go-wrong-for-the-beach-boys/

Carlin, Peter A. (2006). *Catch a wave: The rise, fall, and redemption of the Beach Boys' Brian Wilson*. Emmaus, PA: Rodale Books.

Chidester, B. (2014). Busy doin' something: Uncovering Brian Wilson's lost bedroom tapes. *Paste*, 7 March. https://www.pastemagazine.com/articles/2014/03/busy-doin-somethin-uncovering-brian-wilsons-lost-b.html?p=2

Chidester, B. (2014). Brian Wilson's secret bedroom tapes. *LA Weekly*, 30 January. https://www.laweekly.com/music/brian-wilsons-secret-bedroom-tapes-4392791

Chidester, B. (2014). Brian Wilson's secret bedroom tapes: A track-by-track description. *LA Weekly*, 5 March. https://www.laweekly.com/music/brian-wilsons-secret-bedroom-tapes-a-track-by-track-description-4479099

D'Arcangelo, S. (2018). The Beach Boys announce summer tour. *Live for Live Music*, 24 May. https://liveforlivemusic.com/news/beach-boys-summer-tour-2018/

Dillon, M. (2012). *Fifty sides of the Beach Boys: The songs that tell their story*. Toronto: ECW Press.

Giles, J. (2016). That time the Beach Boys tried to pull it together for *Surf's Up*. *Ultimate Classic Rock*, 30 August. http://ultimateclassicrock.com/beach-boys-surfs-up/

Holdship, B. (2000). *The Beach Boys: An American Family*: Heroes and villains. *LA New Times*, 4 June.

Ingham, J. (1973). The Beach Boys #2: The exiles return. *New Musical Express*, 31 March.

Kent, N. (1975). Brian Wilson: The last great beach movie, Part 3. *New Musical Express*, 12 July.

Locey, B. (2005). Leader of the jam: Music vet Ray Kennedy lords over a freewheeling, fun evening of classic rock in Agoura Hills. Raymondlouiskennedy.com, 13 January. https://web.archive.org/web/20081007000342/http:/www.raymondlouiskennedy.com/new.html

Love, M., & Hirsch, J. S. (2016). *Good vibrations: My life as a Beach Boy*. New York: Blue Rider Press.

Oving, R. (2009). Beach Boys in de polder. Transcription of episode of TV show *Andere Tijden [Other Times]*, VPRO/NTR, 4 April. https://anderetijden.nl/aflevering/283/Beach-Boys-in-de-polder

Partridge, K. (2015). Why a comprehensive Beach Boys biopic would likely fail. *Consequence of Sound*, 4 June. https://consequenceofsound.net/2015/06/why-a-comprehensive-beach-boys-biopic-would-likely-fail/

Rensin, D. (1976). Brian Wilson: A conversation with Brian Wilson. *OUI*, December issue.

Wilson, B., & Greenman, B. (2016). *I am Brian Wilson*. New York: Random House.

129/Matinee Idyll

Apter, J. (2010). *Together alone: The story of the Finn brothers*. North Sydney, AU: William Heinemann Australia.

Archives New Zealand (2018). What more could poor Split Enz do? https://www.facebook.com/notes/archives-new-zealand/what-more-could-poor-split-enz-do/2021319574597982/

Bourke, C. (2011). *Blue smoke: The lost history of New Zealand popular music, 1918-1964*. Auckland, NZ: Auckland University Press.

Chunn, M. (1992). *Stranger than fiction: The life and times of Split Enz*. Wellington, NZ: GP Publications.

Dix, John (2005). *Stranded in paradise: New Zealand rock and roll, 1955-1988*. London: Penguin Books.

Hunt, T. (2003). The beginning of the Enz. *Dominion Post*, 19 November. http://www.stuff.co.nz/dominion-post/culture/9407530/The-beginning-of-the-Enz

Johnstone, A. (2015). The life and times of Phil Judd, part 1. *In Deep Conversations* [podcast]. https://soundcloud.com/in-deep-conversations

Spittle, G. (1997). *Counting the beat: A history of New Zealand song*. Wellington, NZ: GP Publications.

Stiggs, B. (2018). The Buster Stiggs story. Modelsband.com, 16 January. https://modelsband.com/the-buster-stiggs-story/

Sutcliffe, P. (1976). Split Enz: The Enz justify the means. *Sounds*, 25 December.

The True Wheel

Author interview with Larry Heinemann of Music for Enophiles, April 2018.

Berman, J. (2007). 1974: Brian Eno, Taking Tiger Mountain By Strategy. *Tiny Mixtapes*, 6 April. https://www.tinymixtapes.com/delorean/brian-eno-taking-tiger-mountain-strategy

Demorest, S. (1975). Eno: The monkey wrench of rock creates happy accidents on Tiger Mt. *Circus*, April issue.

Gill, A. (1998). Brian Eno: To infinity and beyond. *MOJO*, June issue.

Goldman, V. (1977). Eno: Extra natty orations. *Sounds*, 5 February.

Gross, M. (1979). Brian Eno: Mind over music. *Chic*, July issue.

Hilsinger, D. (2004). Doug's story. Saucefaucet.com. http://www.saucefaucet.com/dug_notes.html

MacDonald, I. (1977). Eno Part 1: Before and after science – accidents will happen. *New Musical Express*, 26 November.

Miles (1976). Eno: Zing! go the strings of my art. *New Musical Express*, 27 November.

O'Brien, G. (1978). Eno at the edge of rock. *Interview*, June issue.

Patterson, T. (2017). Oblique strategies. *Shindig!*, October issue.

Salewicz, C. (1974). Announcement: Texans like steak, oil-wells, large hats, and Eno. *New Musical Express*, 7 December.

Sheppard, D. (2009). *On some faraway beach: The life and times of Brian Eno*. Chicago: Chicago Review Press.

Acknowledgements

The starting point for this project was an email from Greg Healey, fellow writer for *Shindig!* magazine and also a book author: "Helloooo! Do you want to write a book?" I'm very grateful to Greg for recognizing the potential of a Song Book book, and for encouraging me to get in touch with Teddie Dahlin, managing director of New Haven Publishing. Thanks so much to Teddie for commissioning the book and for all her practical and logistical guidance.

As mentioned in the Introduction, Jon "Mojo" Mills and Andy Morten at *Shindig!* Magazine had the initial idea for the Song Book feature, and gave me the opportunity to contribute to that feature in the magazine. Jon and Andy are both remarkably committed to carrying out their vision for *Shindig!*, and I feel privileged to be part of that adventure. They've also been hugely supportive of this book, as have my other colleagues at *Shindig!*. Thanks too to Andy for his cover design.

It has been an interesting and unusual experience balancing the work on this book with the responsibilities of a full-time job in a completely different field. I very much appreciate the support I've received from friends and co-workers who, instead of saying "You're doing WHAT?", thought the whole thing was fantastic and who offered their encouragement. I'm also grateful to my family: my mother Carol, my father Mike, and my brother Michael.

My husband, Tom Barrett, has been incredibly tolerant of the late nights and long weekends that working on this book has entailed. He also possesses a sharp editorial eye that has improved the manuscript tremendously. I'm very lucky.

About the Author

Fiona McQuarrie has been writing about music, regularly and irregularly, for more than three decades. She was formerly a music critic at the *Vancouver Sun* and *Province* newspapers, and at *Monday* magazine in Victoria, British Columbia. She has also worked as a freelance music writer, most recently for *Shindig!* magazine. In her other life she is a professor of organizational studies at a Canadian university. She lives near Vancouver, Canada.

Lightning Source UK Ltd.
Milton Keynes UK
UKHW022136180119
335672UK00004B/26/P